Knowing Me Knowing God

D1005503

Knowing Me Knowing God

Exploring Your Spirituality with Myers-Briggs

MALCOLM GOLDSMITH

Abingdon Press
Nashville

KNOWING ME, KNOWING GOD

Copyright © 1997 by Abingdon Press

All rights reserved.

No part of this work may be reproduced or transmitted in any form or by any means, electronic or mechanical, including photocopying and recording, or by any information storage or retrieval system, except as may be expressly permitted by the 1976 Copyright Act or in writing from the publisher. Requests for permission should be addressed to Abingdon Press, P.O. Box 801, 201 Eighth Avenue South, Nashville, TN 37202-0801.

This book is printed on acid-free paper.

Library of Congress Cataloging–in–Publication Data

Goldsmith, Malcolm, 1939–
    Knowing me, knowing God : exploring your spirituality with Myers-Briggs / Malcolm Goldsmith.
        p.   cm.
    Includes bibliographical references (p.   ).
    ISBN 0-687-01705-X (alk. paper)
        1. Pastoral psychology. 2. Myers-Briggs Type Indicator.
    3. Typology (Psychology)—Religious aspects—Christianity.
    I. Title.
    BV4012.2.G65   1997   97-8989
    253.5'2—dc21   CIP

All Bible quotations, unless otherwise noted, are taken from *The Holy Bible, New International Version.* Copyright © 1973, 1978, 1984 by the International Bible Society. Published by Hodder and Stoughton.

ISBN-13: 978-0-6870-1705-8

08 09 10 11 - 14 13 12 11

MANUFACTURED IN THE UNITED STATES OF AMERICA

For Marion, whose experiences of prayer have been so different from mine.

My thanks are due to . . .
. . . my wife, who read through the original script, exercised her T and J and reduced its length by half . . . Philip Law at SPCK who originally suggested the idea and encouraged me when my spirit flagged . . . Paul Slater and Martin Wharton with whom I have shared so many of these ideas over the last few years . . . John and Jane Archer who enabled me to press on . . . and to Tom and Kate who have provided countless reasons for continuing.

Contents

Foreword

I t is now eight years since I was first introduced to the Myers-Briggs Type Indicator. The more I have worked with the theory, the more I have been impressed by the insights it offers into our personalities and behavior. Many of those with whom I have shared these insights in workshops have found illumination and an understanding of some of the confusions they had lived with for years. I suppose I have been so impressed because that has been my own experience too. Some use the Indicator to awaken themselves to new possibilities in their lives and relationships, others for personal insight and growth. It helps our desire to know and understand ourselves, and our relationships with others, with God, and with all of life.

Within the theory of Myers-Briggs, no one personality type is better than any other. There are only different personalities—each with their own particular strengths and weaknesses. And different personalities need different spiritualities. Although this might seem obvious, I wonder how far it is realized in our churches.

Malcolm Goldsmith in this very readable book reminds us how individual and how unique we are, and that our uniqueness affects all we do—including prayer. His intention is to help us learn about our personalities and to use that self-knowledge to enhance our spiritual lives. "Self-knowledge is so important that even if you were raised right up to the heavens, I should like you never to relax your cultivation of it," wrote St. Teresa of Avila.

There is always a danger, in the spiritual life, that we try to model ourselves on others. Not even Jesus was given to us to imitate literally. The New Testament Christ does not say "Imitate me," but "In the way I have loved you, love one another." As Jung says, "To imitate Christ means to live out our own individual destiny as authentically and wholeheartedly as He lived out his."

Malcolm Goldsmith, with typical honesty, encourages us to start from where we are rather than from where we think we ought to be in our spiritual lives. In order to help understand where we start from, he provides an interesting Spirituality Questionnaire, and I can envisage this becoming the starting point for many a discussion. He encourages us to pray out of who we are, out of our own desires, feelings, experiences, and needs. He urges us to bring all that we are to God, to open up to God all our inner rooms, including those we rarely enter or even admit to occupying. This requires courage, a readiness to be vulnerable, and a willingness to trust in God, because we are uniquely precious. It is, of course, a lifelong process, but we can take small steps on our individual journeys and grow into the true self God calls us to become.

One of the joys of this book is that it does not preach. It does not insist. It does not pretend to offer final answers. Rather it invites questioning, it encourages experimentation. It is unlike almost all other books on prayer, because it is not written by an Introvert. In the ordinary course of events ENTPs do not write about prayer—but this one has done! Malcolm gives us permission to explore and offers an open, searching, and honest study to help our exploration. It is a gift from the author. I pray that his words may become flesh in many who seek a deeper engagement and union with God through prayer. Perhaps especially for those who believe with Dag Hammarskjold that "the road to holiness passes through the world of action."

Above all we are reminded that we can't grow in the spiritual life by reading books about it. We learn to pray by praying. We learn to love by loving.

Martin Wharton
Bishop of Kingston upon Thames, England

Prologue

What is a Christian to do when prayer seems to make little sense? What is a Christian to do if ordained, and so pledged to a life of discipleship within the disciplines of the church, yet finding that the liturgies and prayers of the church fail to sustain or enlarge an understanding of God?

I have struggled with prayer for many years. I have tried getting up at 5:30 A.M. for an hour or two in prayer, Bible reading, and reflection; daily prayer within a community; following books; trying new patterns; social action and engagement; disengagement and retreats. More often than not the end result seemed to be the experience of talking to nothing and hearing a deafening silence in return. I felt like the prophet who said, "truly you are a God who hides yourself."[1]

Despite the poverty of my endeavors, I have remained committed to prayer. For I have, very occasionally and at odd times throughout my life, been conscious of some "otherness" which I know that I have needed to respond to. I can therefore understand and identify with the comment by Dag Hammarskjold, the former Secretary General of the United Nations Organization, when he wrote:

> Once I answered Yes to Someone—or Something. And from that hour I was certain that existence is meaningful and that, therefore, my life, in self-surrender, has a goal.[2]

I do not believe that my inability to pray was caused by a

"lack of faith." I have always wanted to believe even though belief comes to me with difficulty. Like Thomas Merton I believe that the desire to please God does indeed please God, whether that desire is fulfilled or not.[3] I have come to see that somehow my head and my heart have been at odds. I have known, intellectually, what prayer was about, and I have tried to put into practice what I have learned, but somehow there always seemed to be something missing. Whatever that "something" was, I interpreted it as the experience of prayer.

From solitude to mass meeting, from liturgical structure to spontaneity, from adoration to intercession, and from talking to listening, the experience was invariably the same. A nothingness. I carried this non-experience with me in my heart for many years. I would occasionally share it with a friend, but for most of the time I stoically pressed on alone, going through the motions but seldom discovering any content. It was not a mockery, not a form of dishonesty or deception. It was a genuine desire to pray and to be open to the mystery and reality of God, but it was a desire that, by and large, remained unfulfilled.

It came as a surprise to me, and also as something of a relief, to discover that I was not alone. I am finding that a great many people have had the same experience as mine, but they feel that it is somehow unfaithful or disloyal to talk about it. A great process of collusion therefore takes place, rather like the crowd looking at the emperor in his new clothes. I was pleased to read that Gerard Hughes, one of the most respected spiritual guides of today, had shared my difficulties:

> For a long time I thought I was unique in my inability to pray, a conviction confirmed by some sermons and books on the beauty, value and necessity of prayer. Now I spend much of my time listening to people describe their own experience of prayer, and I realise that I am not unique, that the majority of people have a similar experience, each believing that everyone else can pray better than they.[4]

I am sure that these people, like me, know of others who real-

Prologue

ly can and do pray in a most remarkable manner, and whose lives radiate a sense of God's presence. For most of us this experience of prayer remains a closed book. Prayer is one aspect of spirituality. The pages that follow are an attempt to look at spirituality in a fresh way.

1

Spirituality
A Technicolored Dreamcoat?

P rayer is part of a person's spirituality, but what is spirituality? This is a question which seems very simple but which proves to be extremely difficult to answer when the spotlight is turned on it. Workshops on spirituality are very popular today among people in leadership positions in local churches. Despite spending many years in church membership, many people acknowledge that spirituality is a difficult subject. Many Christians have a deep desire to learn more. "When it comes to spirituality" someone said to me, "we are all learners, aren't we?"

Spirituality is far wider an area than most of us normally conceive. Someone defined it to me as "the search for something to assuage the yearning." Spiritual experiences allow us to:

- stand in awe   as when we become aware of something (or Someone) beyond ourselves;
- delight in our senses   as when we enjoy something beautiful—such as art, music, flowers, or scenery; and
- be enlivened   as when we experience love, acceptance, or forgiveness—so that we know we are of worth.

This book is concerned with spirituality, but it can, of necessity, consider only a tiny part of it, and that is the part which might be called religious spirituality—and even then it is only concerned with a very small part of that vast area. We will look at what makes individual people so different from one another; and at how differences in the ways that people perceive the world and relate to it can affect both their understanding of faith and their journey of discipleship.

The desire to explore and learn more about spirituality must lie behind the amazing growth in the popularity of retreats and conferences on the subject in recent years. When I was ordained over thirty years ago retreats tended to be associated with the Catholic wing of the church and were viewed with suspicion or skepticism by many others. That is no longer the case, and today retreat houses are seen as essential resources for the life and work of the church. Perhaps it has something to do with the general loss of confidence that people have in "the secular." They may not be flocking back to the churches but people are no longer assuming that logical, scientific thinking has eliminated the need for the spiritual side of life. There is an openness to the "other," to the mystical or spiritual dimension of life, but interestingly, many of the people who are now searching do not automatically assume that the churches are the place in which to find this other dimension. What have been traditionally called "fringe" religious groups and many different types of "alternatives" are springing up, offering people a way in to new understandings of their daily experiences, of joy and sorrow, and of anguish, and their search for meaning.

The Swiss psychotherapist Carl Jung used to say that he never had a patient in the second half of his or her life whose problem was not ultimately religious. By that he meant that anyone raised in European society, whatever their religious views, had consciously or unconsciously had to face up to ultimate moral, religious, or spiritual issues. Some people were able to deal with these, and they established a framework of belief (be it orthodox or unorthodox). Other people, for a whole variety of reasons, repressed them into their unconscious. There they might lay dormant, emerge in dreams, and/or create havoc at some later time in life.

But what is the nature of this spiritual quest? What is its destiny? What is its process? How do people choose from the vast array of options available? Why are there so many? It seems strange that, with so many people spending time in prayer and contemplation, the way ahead so often seems to be hidden, and so many differing (and often apparently contradictory) practices are followed.

There are many "flavors" to be found among Christian churches today. Within any one denomination there will be a vast range of ways in which people approach biblical interpretation, pray, worship, talk about faith, relate to one another, and expect to experience God's presence and guidance. If we look more widely to include people who do not go to church or profess any faith, we will find just about every point on the continuum which runs from "I don't know what on earth you are talking about" to "the faith which was handed down to me is precious and I have a duty to pass it on in the manner in which I received it." How we account for such differences is, in itself, a reflection of our understanding of and approach to spirituality and faith. It is the argument of this book that these differences in approach and understanding of faith are fundamental to our very being. What we each need to discover is an authentic and meaningful approach to spirituality which we can explore, experience, and maintain without compromising our personal integrity.

For many people, the spiritual quest is about an inward journey. It is an exploration of a mystery in which they discover who they really are. This discovery can only take place as they become more open to the reality and mystery of God. It is deeply personal and it is private. Others discover the reality of God, and probably the reality of themselves, as they engage with other people. They reflect on these experiences and the events of the world and seek to discover their meaning and significance. For them it is less a withdrawal from the world and more an engagement with it which sustains them in their spiritual journey.

Then again, some people need a rational base for their pilgrimage. Suspicious of too much emotion and alert to the possibilities of being overwhelmed by too much "religion" they want to be able to think through their approach to faith. They recognize that they may not be able to reach God by their intellect alone, but they are adamant that they can never be satisfied with a faith which requires them to let go of their intellect and cease their questioning. Yet another group of people needs to feel, above all, an accepting and sustaining relationship with "that which is beyond them." They find encouragement in what other people can offer. For them, the emphasis is likely to be upon their own individual search for meaning and acceptance, and they are more likely to be moved by an appeal to the heart than by an appeal to the head.

Another area where there are differences in approach is in the use and understanding of symbols and visual stimuli. Some people are greatly helped by music, or by colors and even textures, while others may not see their relevance. One person likes incense and another is appalled by it. One person likes to meditate for an hour, perhaps using a candle to focus attention, while another may be totally alienated by the prospect of spending so much time with so little to occupy sight or hearing. It is not that one approach is right and the other is wrong, it is just that they are different. In the same way, people's approach to Scripture may be different. One person may focus quite clearly on specific texts and their precise meaning. Another will use Bible verses as a springboard for developing ideas.

One of the most obvious areas where there is a difference in approach to spirituality today is in "zoning-in" and "opening-up." "Zoning-in" here means focusing upon God by seeking to be freed from all distractions, and laying hold of the central truths and reality of faith by working to free the mind from the thousand and one ideas and thoughts which assail it. This is in sharp contrast to "opening-up" where a person seeks to explore new possibilities, and latches on to the ideas which come to mind to see if they are possible doorways into new understandings or appreciations of God.

With so many possible approaches to the spiritual life, it is not unreasonable to wonder if there is any such thing as an authentic, objective, spiritual journey! Could it be just an illusion? A technicolored dreamcoat? Fascinating, attractive, even seductive, but in the end insubstantial, a figment of our imagination, the sort of thing that dreams are made of?

I suspect that many people ask themselves these questions, because they feel that their own spiritual journey does not correspond to what they hear in sermons, or read in books, or observe in the lives of people whom they respect and admire. My aim in this book is to help you explore the many different experiences of spirituality and to reflect on them in the light of individual personality preferences. The spiritual quest is an important one. People need to be helped to be honest about their experiences. They must work at what is meaningful for them, and not feel that in order to have any validity, their own spirituality must in some way approximate to some sort of blueprint.

An interesting book was published in 1987 entitled Who We Are Is How We Pray,[1] and a similar theme has been explored more recently by Bruce Duncan in Pray Your Way.[2] Both these writers, and a number of others, endeavor to help free us from the shackles that can imprison us when we are made to feel or think that there is a particularly "right" way to pray (and invariably we assume that we have the "wrong" approach). There is a great need for each of us to discover a pathway of spirituality which is appropriate for us individually. It won't necessarily be an easy or straightforward pathway to walk. We may be able to discover a way of praying and reflecting, or thinking and living, which "speaks" to us in our uniqueness, and does not assume that what is right for someone else is therefore automatically right for us. I have discovered that it is a great deal easier to set out with confidence on this journey of exploration if there is a useful guide. Understanding the dynamics of personality can be such a guide. It is clear enough to point a way forward, but flexible and wide enough for us to be able to find our own way without being forced into a specific mold or pattern.

Joseph's technicolored dreamcoat was a gift of love which he wore with pride and assurance. If we can discover a spirituality which can be authentic for us as individuals, then this can be regarded as a gift of love. It will be something precious which we will wear, if not with pride and assurance, then certainly with gratitude and growing confidence.

2 Understanding
Personality Type

There are many different techniques which people can use to begin to understand themselves. Transactional Analysis was very much in vogue in the sixties, emphasizing the different roles that we often adopt in relationships—parent, child, and adult. In recent years many people have been attracted to the Enneagram,[1] which highlights inner drives. However, the Myers-Briggs Type Indicator (MBTI)[2] has become by far the most popular. It is the contribution that the MBTI can make to our understanding of spirituality that this book explores. Readers who already know about MBTI, have attended workshops and explored their own profile may want to skip this chapter and move on to the next section. For those who do not have a working knowledge of the work of Isabel Myers and her mother, or who need a crash revision course, this chapter is designed to introduce the basic concepts. The theory behind the MBTI is explained more fully in my book Knowing Me—Knowing You.[3]

Some people may find this chapter quite heavy going! It may be that you need to read it through two or three times before you begin to feel at home with the ideas. I hope you will persevere, because a great many people have found the idea of personality type a great help when exploring their own spirituality and the spirituality of others.

The Myers-Briggs Type Indicator

It is called a type indicator because it is a process or framework which helps us to differentiate between personality types. The words "Myers-Briggs" are the surnames of the two women, mother and daughter, who devised the indicator. Katharine Cook Briggs was born in Michigan in 1875 and her daughter Isabel was born in 1897; Isabel shared her mother's passion for trying to understand different types of people and their personalities, and together they worked for many years trying to devise a way of describing and categorizing these personalities. In 1923 Carl Jung's book Psychological Types was printed in English and this provided the two women with the theoretical basis that they were looking for. From that time onwards they devoted their lives to exploring and expanding Jung's theories and formulating a way in which these could be incorporated into some form of personality profiling.

It was not until 1975, some sixty years after they had begun working on this, that the Myers-Briggs Type Indicator was published on the open market in the United States, and it immediately made a considerable impact. Isabel Myers wrote Gifts Differing shortly before her death in 1980, and since then the MBTI has become the most widely used personality assessment in the world. It is being used increasingly within the churches to help people understand not only their own personalities and the personalities of others, but also to understand their spiritual explorations and journeys. I have found it to be a great help in exploring spirituality but would want to add the proviso that it is only one aid, among many, and I would not want to suggest that there should be some form of MBTI spirituality cult.

The MBTI theory of personality type hinges on the idea of preference. Jung believed that we are born with innate preferences, and that these affect the ways in which we perceive the world around us, take in information from the world, process it, and develop our responses to it, our actions and behavior. He believed that we operate on the level of our preferences in an unconscious way, and that these preferences become so well developed that we rely on them to enable us to live and cope in a complex world. There are other responses that we could make, and that we sometimes do make, and other processes and functions that operate in our personality, but we find these more difficult, we are less adept at handling them, and we use or prefer them less.

A simple and rather crude example can be taken from our handwriting. When we sign our name, we tend to pick up a pen or pencil and write automatically. We do not stop and ask ourselves which hand to use, or which way our letters should slant, or the style of our writing—we just sign our name. We could, of course, write with our other hand, but in that case we would have to make a conscious effort, and we would find that quite difficult and have to concentrate hard. The end result, in all probability, would be rather untidy and unsatisfactory. We can actually do it, and there may be times when it is appropriate for us to do so—those times when we have strained our wrist or damaged the fingers on our "writing hand" for example—but normally we write with our preferred hand, without thinking, and, over the years, through constant use, our signature has developed and become something special and unique to us.

That simple illustration can represent the whole range of highly complex decisions which we are taking all day long, every day, for the whole of our lives. Two people going into the same building can notice different things, two people having a conversation can remember different things, two people approaching a third person may interact in different ways, two people attending the same church service may respond in different ways, and the same two people, when discussing their career prospects may wish to follow entirely different routes and develop their interests in very different areas. The principal reasons for these differences, according to Jung, are born with us. Now this is obviously highly simplified, and there have to be a great many provisos and caveats. Nevertheless the argument is that people are born with different preferences and the way in which we handle these preferences as we grow up, and the way in which they react with our differing environments all play a part in making us the people that we are.

As we grow, so we develop preferred ways of Perceiving (taking information in) and Judging (deciding on our behavior in the world). Sometimes we feel threatened and under pressure, or we find ourselves in situations where we are expected to behave in certain ways, and we use other processes which may not, in fact, be our preferred ways of acting. We can thus grow up "out of step" with ourselves, and it may be a long and painful journey for us to become reconciled with the person that we "really are"—this will be looked at later in the book.

The theory behind the MBTI goes on to suggest that our behavior (the combination of ways of taking in information, processing it, and developing responses and actions in the world) is not random but follows certain patterns. These patterns are not determined so that they take away our personal responsibility. Instead we remain free to choose how we behave, but we are more likely to act in certain ways because of the preferences which we have developed. I am much more likely to choose a tape or CD of Bach than of the Beatles. That is not to say that I am not free to choose a tape or CD by the Beatles nor that I won't ever choose one, but it is far more likely that I will opt for Bach because that is my preference. People who know me well will begin to know my preferences and so my choices and behavior can be, to a certain degree, anticipated and predicted by them.

Jung, who was a psychoanalyst, tended to be preoccupied with people who deviated from the normal. Isabel Myers and her mother developed and refined Jung's ideas, paying far more attention to the "normality" of people rather than to abnormalities. They were particularly interested in what made people different from each other, and how different people might relate to each other with the minimum of friction and the maximum of understanding. They wanted to help people to grow and develop and to be able to fulfill their potential rather than being stuck as square pegs in the many round holes of life. It is their positive approach to human differences and their valuing of people as unique individuals which makes their Indicator such a useful and appropriate instrument through which to explore spirituality. Our experiences of God, and our longings for God are different and unique to ourselves even though they may sometimes be shared by some other people, but not by all other people.

The Myers-Briggs Type Indicator describes sixteen different personality types and people can eventually be described, often with surprising accuracy, by one of these. However, within each different category there are bound to be differences and placing people in one particular "personality type box" does not destroy their individuality nor their uniqueness. It has been said that people in any particular personality category are like all others in that category, are like some of the others, and are like none of the others! That is, there are certain basic similarities, which distinguish them from other personality types, but which still allow them to be different. The MBTI recognizes and honors those differences.

I find that very often people are quite suspicious about any attempt to place others into categories, thinking that to do so is to take away from those people their own individuality. I can understand such a fear, but I believe that it is an unnecessary one. People attending an international conference might, at some stage, be divided into nationality groups: all the British go to one room, the Germans to another, the French to another, and so on. To divide people in this way is to recognize that they may have many things in common—a common language, similar cultural conditioning, a number of shared experiences—but it does not suggest that they are all the same, nor that they have the same outlook, ideas, or individual histories. Experience shows that there are bonds that unite people across national boundaries, and that there are divisions between people within nationalities—but nevertheless, national groupings are often a very useful and helpful way of dividing people within nationalities—but nevertheless, national groupings are often a very useful and helpful way of dividing people up for certain things. The same is true of personality type.

Isabel Myers made it quite clear in her writings that no one type is any better than any other. Each personality type has specific gifts and insights to offer to others, and each type has certain things which it finds more difficult to come to terms with. Using the MBTI enables people to identify strengths in their own personality. There is a mutual interdependence between types, and it was for this reason that Isabel Myers called her book Gifts Differing and, near its close, could write:

> When people differ, a knowledge of type lessens friction and eases strain. In addition, it reveals the value of differences. No one has to be good at everything. By developing individual strengths, guarding against known weaknesses, and appreciating the strengths of the other types, life will be more amusing, more interesting, and more of a daily adventure that [sic] it could possibly be if everyone were alike.[4]

In this book I am not going to explain these types in detail. I wish to encourage people who are interested in this to attend one of the many workshops that are now available, complete the questionnaire, and receive individual feedback and explanation from a qualified and trained consultant. If you don't know how to find such a workshop in your own locality, Vision, the magazine of the National Association for Promoting Retreats usually has a list of residential courses; if you are not able to attend a residential course, you could contact the leaders of these courses and inquire if they know of any local non-residential courses. In this book I am drawing upon some of the insights gained from the Indicator to illustrate different aspects of spirituality and I invite you to explore your own spiritual journey using this method. On that journey you will recognize the characteristics of different personality types. You will also recognize areas in yourself which you will need to work on if you are to grow in understanding and allow yourself to become more open to God.

How the MBTI Is Built Up

The MBTI has four main components. Our behavior is the result of how we receive information about the world (people, places, and things). This process is one of Perception. It is allied to another component, namely, how we reach decisions. The process by which we reach decisions is one of Judgment. These are technical terms, and imply no value judgment; one is not better than the other.

When we look at the process of perception we are faced with a choice. Some people prefer to rely upon their five senses to provide the bulk of the information they handle—it comes to them through what they see, or hear; what they touch, or smell, or taste. Other people prefer to take in information through what amounts to a "sixth sense"—their intuition, their gut feelings, or hunches. These people tend to have a general view of what is or might be, rather than a specific view of precise details. The first process is known as Sensing and the other as iNtuition. Everyone uses both of these processes, but they actually have a preference for one rather than the other (just as they prefer to write with one hand rather than with the other).

As people prefer to take in information either through Sensing or through iNtuition, so the way in which they deal with this information and come to a conclusion about it is dependent upon another choice. Some people prefer to go through a Thinking route, which means that they tend to be objective and more concerned with principles, while others prefer to follow a Feeling route, which means that they tend to be more subjective and more concerned with harmony and with establishing good relationships. Once again, everyone uses both processes, but they prefer using one to the other. The choice has nothing whatsoever to do with intelligence. The Thinking process is not more intellectual or cleverer than the Feeling process; it is just different.

The third component in the Myers-Briggs Type Indicator concerns where we get our energy and inspiration. Some people are energized by engagement with the outside world. Others gain their strength from their own inner depths, and prefer to have time to themselves, and find that too much engaging with the outer world of people and things and events can be extremely tiring. The former are known in MBTI terms as Extroverts and the latter as Introverts. Again we have to be rather careful about the use of the terms, for in common parlance an "extrovert" tends to be thought of as someone who is rather loud and "bigger than life," which is not quite the same as the more technical meaning given to the word within the MBTI. Everyone operates on both axes, but they prefer one to the other.

Finally we have a preference between what might be called "open" and "closed" lifestyles. Some people like to get things prepared well in advance and they like to know where they stand on a whole range of issues. They value dependability, structure, and loyalty. Other people, however, may prefer to leave things to the last minute. They prefer flexibility and spontaneity, and are likely to change their mind much more easily than the first group. The latter are people who have a preference for a Perceiving lifestyle. The former prefer a Judging approach (again, remember that these are technical terms and they are of equal value and importance; one is not "better" than the other).

So there are four separate axes, and the MBTI theory is that people have a preference for one rather than the other choice on each scale.

1. Extrovert (E)   or   Introvert (I)
   (showing where we get our energy, how we are revitalized)
2. Senser (S)   or   iNtuitive (N)
   (showing how we take in information)
3. Thinker (T)   or   Feeler (F)
   (showing how we process that information)
4. Perceiver (P)   or   Judger (J)
   (showing whether we prefer an "open" or "closed" lifestyle)

Each person has a preference for Extroversion (E) or Introversion (I); for Sensing (S) or iNtuition (N); for Thinking (T) or Feeling (F); and for Judging (J) or Perceiving (P). The combination that each person comes out with, having made these (usually unconscious) choices, will mean that they fit into one of sixteen different categories—sixteen being the number of different combinations you can obtain from four variables. For instance, someone may assess that they are Extrovert, iNtuitive, Thinking, and Judging; and this would be summarized by the letters ENTJ. Someone else may come to the conclusion that they are Introvert, Sensing, Feeling, and Perceiving, and their type would be summarized by the letters ISFP.

It is not the intention of this chapter to explain the theory in great detail. This is just a simple introduction. The important thing is to realize that there are these polarities on the four different processes, and that people have different preferences. It is important to grasp this basic point, as later we shall try to show how different forms of spirituality can reflect or focus upon these differences.

Working Out Your Own Type

- If you are an Extrovert you will tend to be energized by events, situations, or people outside of yourself; whereas if you are an Introvert you will tend to find these tiring and need to gain your strength from deep down within yourself.
- If you are an Extrovert you will tend to speak first, and then think about what you have said—you do your thinking while talking out loud, whereas if you are an Introvert you try to sort out your thoughts in your mind before you speak.
- If you are an Extrovert you probably know lots of people, seem to have a lot of friends, and enjoy being with them, going places and doing things. You are likely to know quite a lot about them—their thoughts and details concerning their personal life. If you are an Introvert you may not know quite so many people, and they certainly will not know too much about you and your personal affairs. You will not "wear your heart on your sleeve." You will probably prefer your own company or that of just one or two very close friends.

All of us are a mixture of both Extrovert and Introvert. In different situations we will tend to be one rather than the other, but we have an innate preference for one, and we are more at home operating in that mode. It is not better to be one rather than the other, they are just different!

- If you are a Senser you probably prefer things to be specific and detailed, whereas if you are an iNtuitive you may well get bored with detail and prefer the broad, generalized picture.
- Sensers like specific, manageable, and possibly separate "blocks" of information, work, or activities. INtuitives prefer them to be all interrelated in some way; they like a "big picture."
- If you are a Senser you will prefer to do something rather than merely think about it, while iNtuitives generally prefer thoughts to actions—and they are often not very good when it comes to being practical.
- Sensers think that "seeing is believing" and prefer things to be grounded and rooted in the present tense. INtuitives, on the other hand, are often more concerned about the future than they are about the present, and they like dreaming and imagining possibilities.
- If you are a Senser you may well have quite a keen eye for color and for detail, whereas if you are an iNtuitive these things can very often pass you by without your noticing them.

We are all a mixture of both Senser and iNtuitive, and at different times we opt for one rather than the other. But we have an innate preference for the one approach which is most normal and usual for us. It is not better to be one rather than the other, they are just different!

- If you are a Thinker, you probably prefer to settle disputes on grounds that are fair and objective rather than on what makes people happy, whereas if you are a Feeler you probably prefer to decide things on the basis of what is likely to be most harmonious.
- If you are a Thinker, processes are important to you and you will tend to believe that you cannot have a good conclusion or end result if it is not built upon good, logical, and reason-

able foundations. If you are a Feeler you just know that what is important is the end result—peace, harmony, acceptance—and that this is more important than being overconcerned about processes.

- If you are a Thinker you tend to be more firm-headed than tenderhearted, while the Feeler would have things the other way round.
- If you are a Thinker you probably prefer to see things from the outside, as an onlooker, while Feelers tend to prefer to see situations from the inside, as though they themselves were involved.

We are all both Thinkers and Feelers, and at different times we operate in different ways. But we actually have a basic preference for one rather than the other, and that is what we naturally return to. It is not better to be one rather than the other, they are just different!

- If you are a Judger, you are usually on time for appointments and prefer things to have their own time and place. Perceivers, on the other hand, are more likely to be late—possibly because they couldn't find whatever it was that they were looking for!
- If you are a Judger you probably make lots of lists, and keep to them, whereas Perceivers don't think in terms of lists, or if they do, they seldom keep to them.
- Judgers tend to appreciate organizations, hierarchies, rules, and regulations (not necessarily for their own sake, but because they allow and enable things to happen, to be achieved). Perceivers get bored with institutions, and with set procedures and formalized structures. They prefer a more informal and autonomous climate.
- Judgers like things to be well organized, and they like to know where they stand in relation to situations. Perceivers are more likely to "fly by the seat of their pants," see most things as being provisional, and are always prepared to change their minds if something else seems more appropriate.

We all operate, at different times, in both modes but we have a natural preference for one rather than the other. It is not better to be one rather than the other, they are just different!

With this information you will probably by now have come to a tentative conclusion as to what your type is and be able to put four letters together which summarize it. If you are not able to do this at the moment, do not worry! It is more important that you realize what is going on, and the differences that exist, than that you are able to make a precise evaluation of your own position.

One reason why the Myers-Briggs Type Indicator has become so popular in recent years is that it helps people to appreciate their strengths and recognize their weaknesses. It can help them to understand why they find certain tasks difficult, or why certain people always seem to irritate them, and it can help them to appreciate how other people "tick." It can be very helpful in exploring the ways in which people relate to each other, whether this is in a family, in a work situation, or in a church. It can help in understanding how committees work, and in how to communicate more effectively with different people. (All these subjects are dealt with more fully in Knowing Me—Knowing You, mentioned earlier.)

A Little More Theory

Our personalities are complex and dynamic, and there is always the danger when simplifying things of giving the impression that we are static and easily described and divided up into clear manageable compartments. The truth, of course, is rather different! I now want to look at how we might consider the four letters that describe our personality type in such a way as to give them greater depth and a sense of movement. Our behavior is the result of a combination of judging and perceiving functions. That means that we prefer thinking or feeling processes and these react with our preference for sensing or intuitive processes. We are energized either by the external world and its events or by our own inner world of thoughts and reflections.

Understanding

This can be summarized diagrammatically in the following way:

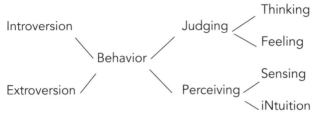

We now need to explore the interrelationship between all these parts, and to see how what can appear as a rather daunting diagram can actually "come alive."

Our behavior (or the behavior that we observe in other people)—whether this is in our working life, our domestic or church life, or in our friendships with other people—is the result of how we perceive the world around us, how we take in information about it, and then how we assemble and use that information.

Every personality has what is known as a dominant function that is more influential in shaping it, and this is partnered by what is known as the auxiliary function. I will give an illustration of what I mean because many people find this a difficult part of the theory to understand.

Imagine four people standing in a row and speaking at the same time. One person is shouting, another person is speaking rather loudly, the third has a fairly quiet speaking voice, and the fourth one is barely audible, there is just a whisper. The likelihood is that you will immediately hear what the shouter is communicating, and with a little care you will probably also be able to focus your attention on the loud voice as well, being able to hear that message separately. The quieter voice and the whisper will be very difficult to distinguish. In much the same way the different functions which make up our personality are also "speaking" and some of them are "louder" than others, and tend to dominate our personality.

Every personality has what is known as a dominant function which is more influential than the others in shaping it. This will be one of the two central letters in our MBTI personality profile. Thus, if I am an ENTJ it will be either N or T, if I am an ISFP it will be either S or F, and so forth. The other central letter is known as the auxiliary function. For example, someone who is ENTP has a dominant N and an auxiliary T; someone who is an ISTJ has a dominant S and an auxiliary T; a person who is an ESTP has a dominant S and auxiliary T; and an INFP has a dominant F and an auxiliary N. On first sight, such illustrations may seem obvious, but on second sight they may confuse you as there appears to be no definite pattern, apart from finding the dominant and auxiliary in the central two letters. How do we know which is the dominant and which is the auxiliary? If a person is an ENTP, how do we know whether the dominant is N or T, as they are both central letters in the profile?

To do this we have to take note of the first and last letters in our four-letter profile, as they determine how we settle on which is the dominant and auxiliary. So, in our example of ENTJ, we need to look at the E and J, as they provide the clue as to whether the dominant is N or T.

The final letter of each set of four (J or P) points to the function that we use in the outer world; the function that is seen by others. If the final letter is a J it will tell us that the outer world is addressed by our T or F—because both these are "Judging functions" and having a J at the end tells us that we show a Judging function to the outer world. If the final letter is a P then we know that what is shown to the world is either S or N—because both those are Perceiving functions and therefore having a P at the end tells us that we show a Perceiving function to the outer world. In our example of ENTJ we can now say that the J tells us that this person uses their T in the outer world—that is what other people will notice about them.

That was looking at the final letters of J or P. Now let us look at the first letters—E or I. If a person is an Extrovert then that person shows their "best" to the outer world; they are at home in it, energized by it, and like to relate and react to it. If, however, a person is an Introvert, then they place a greater value on their inner world and are more at home with that, finding the outer world rather more threatening or difficult to deal with. Thus, if the first letter in a personality profile is an E, then we know that what they show to the outer world will be their dominant function, and what is kept close in, to themselves, will be their auxiliary. If the first letter in a profile is an I, then we know that person will keep their dominant to themselves, as it were, and what is shown to the outer world is their auxiliary.

The second letter of the four in the MBTI profile is the dominant for E—Ps and I—J's; while the third letter of the four is the dominant for E—Js and I—Ps. In the examples which follow, the dominant function has been highlighted:

ESTJ   INFJ   ISTP   ENTP   ISFP   ESFP   ISFJ

See if you can pick out which is the dominant in the following types:

ESFP   INTJ   ENFJ   INFP   ESFJ   ENFP   ISTJ[5]

Everyone has both a dominant and an auxiliary function, and these always work together to produce a dynamic personality, which has movement and life. In our earlier example, where four people were in a line, shouting, talking loudly, talking quietly, and whispering, the dominant and the auxiliary were the two loudest voices in the line.

Even More Theory!

It is also possible to speak about the tertiary (or third) and fourth functions. In our example of four voices, these would be the two quieter ones, the ones which we hardly notice because of the strength of the other two. The tertiary and fourth functions are also known as the least-preferred or inferior functions and other people talk about them as the shadow. These are the opposites to the auxiliary and dominant (and so are not shown in the four letter profiles—because they are the other end of the scale of the two central letters). Thus, if a person's personality has a dominant N, which means that this is the function which is most influential in shaping that personality, then because S is at the other end of the S–N axis, Sensing will be the least-preferred function. If the auxiliary is the second most influential, then the opposite end of that axis will give us the tertiary or third preference. The concept of least-preferred functions is a crucial area when dealing with spirituality, and chapter 5 will be devoted to it.

It is quite important for us to be able to identify our dominant function (but don't despair if, at this stage it all seems too complicated for you!), because although we use all four functions (Sensing, iNtuition, Thinking, and Feeling), and have done so all our life, we do not use them in equal measure and have not developed them all to the same degree. We are therefore happier using one rather than another, and we are less clumsy, less embarrassed, and find it less tiring when we use our dominant and auxiliary rather than our third and fourth, less-preferred or inferior functions.

For ease, our personality profile is usually given as four letters (ISTJ, ENTP, INFP, and so forth). To be precise we could say that it really contains six letters, and we could indicate it as follows (using ENTP as an example):

$$
\begin{array}{ccc}
& E & \\
N & & T \\
F & & S \\
& P &
\end{array}
$$

For an ENTP, being an Extrovert: the dominant is N, the auxiliary T, the tertiary (third) function is F, and the least-preferred (fourth) function is S, within an approach which is Perceiving. Such a formula would be very cumbersome, and (once we have seen how it is done) we can work out the least-preferred (or inferior) functions from the information that we already have.

The MBTI theory suggests (although there is still debate about this) that when we extrovert our dominant then we introvert the other three functions, and when we introvert our dominant then we extrovert the other three functions. By this I mean that when we extrovert, or project onto the outer world our dominant function, then we tend to internalize, make private, and guard the other three functions, and vice versa. To extrovert a function is to display it, as it were, to "wear it on our sleeve," while to introvert a function is to turn it inward and make it more difficult for others to recognize it. It will be helpful to remember this when we turn to look at spirituality and how our personality affects the ways in which we understand God or interpret our experiences of God. This also helps us to understand how different people prefer different approaches to God, or enjoy different types and styles of worship, and prefer to belong to one type of congregation rather than another.

MBTI and Christian Faith

Although the MBTI is not a specifically Christian instrument, it is one of many helpful tools that are available for Christians to use. Writing about Isabel Briggs Myers, her son Peter said that she

> was not a member of any religious denomination but throughout her life demonstrated a deep and abiding faith in her Creator and a loving concern and respect for all of God's creatures . . . she felt that there was more than enough adversity in the world and she dreamed of helping people to help themselves by concentrating on the positive, by recognising and appreciating their gifts, and by understanding and valuing human differences.[6]

It may come as a surprise to some people to realize that other people perceive and experience God in different ways, and to acknowledge that what supports and encourages one person in their spiritual journey may have no effect whatsoever upon someone else. What one person finds helpful may positively discourage another. Understanding personality type can be a very helpful tool in this process of discovery, but it is not the only instrument, and it should not be presumed that understanding type will automatically develop your spiritual life and that there will be little need of anything else. Nor should it ever be thought that a person's spiritual life cannot be fully developed without them coming to terms with Myers Briggs!

Knowing Me, Knowing God

There were millions of saints, living exemplary lives, long before Jung's ideas were developed by Katharine Briggs and Isabel Myers, and there are many alive today who have never heard of Jung and do not understand the meaning of personality type but who have discovered an authentic pattern of spirituality which we can only respect and admire. Nevertheless, there are others for whom the insights offered by this particular approach have been helpful, stimulating, and occasionally liberating. This book uses the Myers-Briggs Type Indicator as a framework for exploring spirituality, but the emphasis is very much upon exploring. Be prepared for wrong turnings, blind alleys, mistakes, and recapitulations! The journey will probably prove to be interesting, stimulating, and illuminative, but I cannot guarantee it. Each person must discover his or her own spiritual identity and what feeds and sustains it, for themselves. No one else can set out definitive rules or instructions which are necessarily right for you. Each one of us has to discover them for ourself, but we can be helped along the way by the insights and experiences of others.

There are questions that Christians occasionally raise when confronted by the MBTI approach. I have heard it said that Christians should not delve into such things, as they are somehow dangerous and tied up with the occult. Well, anything can be dangerous if it is misused, or if it is misunderstood and inappropriately applied. "A little learning is a dangerous thing," the saying goes, but there is nothing dangerous or suspicious about the idea of personality, nor of this particular approach to it. It has nothing to do with occult practices or superstition, and it is based upon many years of solid research and intellectual questioning. As I have already pointed out, it is not a specifically Christian instrument any more than a motor car, word processor, or electric light, but like those examples many Christians use it and have been helped by it.

Some people suggest that it is too trendy and could be used by churches to "replace the Gospel." There is always a danger that something can become too popular and develop overenthusiastic fans, and no doubt this approach to spirituality can suffer from such overzealous supporters—but that would be to ignore the cautions that I have already given! The instrument makes no claims to be anything more than a help, a tool, available for people to use in order to enlarge their understanding of themselves and others. Perhaps it can make them more sensitive, and offer possible ways of tackling issues and people that they find difficult.

It has also been suggested by some people that it is dangerous to stereotype and determine people, placing them in boxes and telling them what they are like, and that it is wrong to probe into people's personal space. All this is true, but if such an objection is made to the MBTI it is to misunderstand what it is all about. The Indicator does not prejudge or determine people, nor does it place people in watertight compartments (perhaps against their will), and reveal to others things that are private and deeply personal. The Indicator is self-determining, by which I mean that you yourself are the person who decides which "profile" fits you most easily. No one ever puts you into a category that you do not want to be in, and nothing about you is revealed to others that you have been trying to keep secret. What is offered is a framework which helps you to understand and use more creatively things about yourself and others which are already known. Anyone is free to change their minds about their personality profile at any time, and indeed, as people grow older they often begin to appreciate little changes that seem to take place—they often grow more reflective and more introverted, for example.

Finally, I have heard it suggested that the Indicator leaves "no room for God." On one workshop I was leading a lady became very distressed at one stage and claimed that I was "not allowing room for the Holy Spirit to work." There is absolutely no truth in the suggestion that such an Instrument seeks to "play God" or that it takes away the space and possibilities that might be used by God. Commenting on this sort of fear Mark Pearson, an American Episcopalian priest who is President of the Institute for Christian Renewal, has written:

> When God goes to work making us holier people, He does not destroy the personality we have. He transforms it. . . . The Peter

of the Gospels is spiritually immature. But in the Acts of the Apostles, by which time the Holy Spirit has accomplished some spiritual growth in Peter, we don't suddenly find an introvert mystic. We find the same extrovert, plain-spoken man, but with maturity. God didn't give Peter a different personality. God improved the personality He had already given him . . . [God says] "My child, I gave you this personality as My special gift. I knew you before I formed you in your mother's womb (Jeremiah 1.5; Psalm 139.13). Just as your eye color and the shape of your ears are a part of how I made you, so is your per-sonality. It is something I gave you; thus, there is no personality type that is better or worse than another. Any personality type can be used for My glory or can be an expression of rebellion to Me. Yes, you have misused it. You need to come to Me for forgiveness and you need to let the Holy Spirit mature you. Yes, it has been wounded because of the sin of others. I don't want to give you a different personality. If you were supposed to have a different personality, I would have given you that one in the first place. What I want to do is make you a better version of who you already are."[7]

3
A Spirituality Questionnaire

I t is clear that different people have different preferences, and that these are not "right" or "wrong," but just different. I may prefer football to rugby, Bach to the Beatles, and ice-cream to yogurt. Someone else may prefer Sears to Nieman Marcus, Cliff Richards to Frank Sinatra, and Maine to Colorado. People are free to have their preferences, and they make the world a richer and more interesting place in which to live. This book considers how people's preferences operate in the world of spirituality. The questionnaire in this chapter is designed to illustrate this.

Before embarking on the questionnaire, there are some words of caution which need to be heeded. The "profile" which emerges at the end may well not be the same as the personality profile which has been established by taking the full MBTI, and it needs to be stressed that this spirituality questionnaire does not provide an alternative to your "true type." There may be differences in the "profile" which emerge for a number of reasons:

- This spirituality questionnaire is not sufficiently well developed. It took Isabel Myers and her mother many years to develop their questionnaire. That was tested on literally thousands of people, and great care was taken to ensure that each question was properly balanced and weighted so that it only related to one of the functions and could not be applied to another by mistake. The spirituality questionnaire here is far cruder. It is included only as an illustrative tool, for interest, and not as any sort of research instrument.

- When answering questions about the church and spiritual matters it is probable that people are overinfluenced by their past experiences, and so what eventually emerges is a "profile" that has been warped by years of thinking and doing things in a particular way. We become steeped in a particular tradition, and even though that may not be what we would choose if we were "starting from scratch" we may well tend to "go with the stream" of our past experiences.

- We may also be particularly influenced by our own congregation and its culture and outlook. Work is still in the very early stages of exploring whether the MBTI can be applied to organizations, but it would seem likely that just as individual people have their own particular type profile, so organizations may develop a corporate profile.[1] This could therefore mean that when answering certain of the questions, rather than one's "true type" coming out, the answer is unduly influenced by the culture (the ideas, outlook, and style) of the church to which a person belongs.

- When thinking about spiritual issues, it is more likely that many people explore them, not with their dominant processes, but with what is often called their "shadow." This is an important point to make and chapter 5 will explore this later.

When Answering the Questionnaire

1. Look at each question in turn and choose which of the alternatives you prefer. You may agree with both options, but force yourself to make a choice, to state a preference. Choosing one option does not imply that the other option is wrong or that you have no sympathy with it.

2. If you prefer alternative a place a check mark in the little box alongside that number in the grid on page 54 and if you prefer alternative b place a check mark inside that little box. Do not place a check mark in both boxes. Choose between a or b. You may find it difficult to answer a question, but try to make a decision and state a preference.

A Spirituality Questionnaire

3. When you have completed all sixty questions, add up the number of check marks along each vertical column, and put that number in the total box at the foot of the table. Only when you have done all this, transfer the numbers to the chart on page 117.

Using the Questionnaire

This questionnaire is designed for personal completion as an integral part of this book. It can, however, be used in small groups to stimulate discussion. In these cases it is the discussion itself which is important, and it is not necessary to add up the scores nor to work on interpreting them.

THE QUESTIONNAIRE

The answer grid for you to complete is at the end of the chapter

1. Do you prefer Christian faith to
     a. expand your love for the whole of creation
        or
     b. challenge your inner being?

2. When listening to sermons, do you prefer them to
     a. explain and expound the meaning of particular biblical passages
        or
     b. use the Bible as a starting-point for an exploration of contemporary issues?

3. When listening to a sermon, do you prefer
     a. your heart to be warmed
        or
     b. your head to be challenged?

4. Which of these sentences describes you best?
     a. I like services to start on time and finish when I expect them to
        or
     b. I don't mind services starting late, and they finish when they finish!

5. When there are periods of silence in services, do you find that
     a. they last too long and you are never sure when they are going to finish
        or
     b. they are invariably too short?

6. When thinking about your local church,
     a. could you describe in detail its inside—what the windows show, the memorial stones, significant

dates in its history, and the name of the hymnbook you use

or

b. do you tend not to notice details like this; rather,
you are aware of an overall effect but would find
it difficult to describe particulars?

7. When speaking to a preacher after a service, are you
more likely to
   a. say "Thank you"

   or

   b. raise questions about something that was said?

8. **a.** Do you think that the death and resurrection of Jesus
   have a clear and unambiguous meaning

   or

   b. do you think that there are a variety of meanings
   and interpretations which may be valid?

9. Do you find it
   a. reasonably easy and natural to talk to strangers
   who may be visiting your church

   or

   b. quite difficult to know what to say to visitors?

10. Do you prefer sermons
    a. to work systematically through a series of biblical
    themes

    or

    b. to talk about novels, films, plays, and controver-
    sial subjects and how they relate to the gospel?

11. What is more important for a church congregation—
    a. to be a fellowship, accepting one another without
    questions

    or

    b. to be honest searchers after truth, even though
    this may be quite painful for some people?

12. Do you think that
    a. the church should proclaim the historic faith

which has been handed down to it
        or that

b. every age and situation may require a different response from the church?

13. Do you find it
    a. relatively easy to spend time alone in prayer
        or
    b. quite difficult maintaining a personal prayer life?

14. When thinking about your church (the building and congregation), do you
    a. tend to look for minor modifications (but you are basically happy with the way that things are)
        or
    b. dream about totally reordering the inside and making radical alterations to the way that things are?

15. Which do you find the more acceptable when leading worship
    a. a minister who is a nice person but a terrible preacher
        or
    b. a minister who is a good preacher but whom you don't particularly warm to as a person?

16. Do you prefer sermons which
    a. give you specific details and proclaim "the truth"
        or
    b. open up a whole range of possibilities for you to think about?

17. Which of these phrases speaks most immediately to you of God—
    a. "God was in Christ reconciling the world to himself"
        or
    b. "Be still and know that I am God"?

18. Do you prefer

a. facts and figures and things that make sense

or

b. ideas, concepts, and imagining possibilities?

19. Which appeals to you most—
    a. warmth

    or

    b. clarity?

20. When thinking about services, do you
    a. like to know what you can expect, preferring a more traditional approach

    or

    b. like change and variety?

21. When you walk into a strange church, say on vacation, do you prefer to find
    a. evidence of a gospel engagement with the issues of the world

    or

    b. a sense of quietness and retreat from the pressures of the world?

22. What do you prefer to get from worship—
    a. a variety of colors, shapes, smells, or experiences

    or

    b. a variety of ideas?

23. Following an interesting sermon, would you rather
    a. talk about it with a small group of friends

    or

    b. talk to the preacher seeking clarification on points you may have misunderstood?

24. Do you think
    a. that there are basic, nonnegotiable truths which people have to hold on to

    or

    b. that the truth always has to be discovered afresh by each generation in its own way?

25. **a.** Do you know lots of people in your local church, and do they really know you and your story

or

b. do you tend not to know all that many people very well, and feel that your story is a very personal thing?

26. What do you look for in a minister?

a. practicality and being "down to earth"

or

b. vision and idealism

27. When you think about your congregation

a. are you aware of many of the problems that people carry with them concerning themselves and their families

or

b. are you not particularly aware of the problems most of them have?

28. In the conduct of worship do you

a. think that people should be "duly authorized" before they take a leading role in services

or

b. do you think that anyone (and everyone?) should be encouraged to share in leading services?

29. Which of these statements most closely describes your reaction if asked to go on a silent retreat for three or four days?

a. I would be very apprehensive and perhaps reluctant

or

b. The idea is very appealing

30. Which of these qualities do you most admire?

a. perseverance

or

b. enthusiasm

31. When you think of your church leaders, are you more

aware of their
- **a.** strengths

    or
- **b.** weaknesses?

32. What do you value most in your spiritual life
    - **a.** order

        or
    - **b.** spontaneity?

33. Which word best describes the religious life?
    - **a.** fellowship

        or
    - **b.** solitude

34. When confronted by new ideas in theology, mission, or church life, do you tend to
    - **a.** be cautious of them until you find out whether they are true

        or
    - **b.** welcome them until you discover that they are false?

35. If you could only use one word, which of these words would you want to use?
    - **a.** peace

        or
    - **b.** justice

36. Do you think that, in general terms
    - **a.** church rules and tradition should guide our pastoral work

        or
    - **b.** pastoral opportunities should take precedence over church order and tradition?

37. Which of these statements best summarizes your preferences?
    - **a.** I need many things to awaken my sense of God's presence

        or

b. I need a still focal point to help me be aware of God's presence

38. Do you think that giving to projects overseas should
    a. come after the needs of the local church—its mission, outreach, buildings, etc.—have been attended to
    or
    b. take priority over spending on your own church?

39. When conflict arises in your congregation, do you tend to feel that
    a. this is a failure of Christian love, and is greatly to be regretted
    or
    b. this is an inevitable part of being human, and may be creative?

40. When thinking about mission and evangelism, which of these phrases gives most problems—
    a. "No man comes to the Father but through me"
    or
    b. "In my Father's house are many rooms"?

41. Which do you prefer—
    a. a well-attended service, with hymns and many people participating
    or
    b. a very quiet service, perhaps with fewer people attending, where you are "left alone" with your thoughts?

42. When you hear people say that we now live in a multi-faith society, do you first of all think that this
    a. seriously challenges the churches, who must be vigilant not to compromise their faith
    or
    b. offers all sorts of new opportunities to the churches for working together with people of other faiths?

43. When babies or children cry during a service, do you
    a. feel that it is good to have the whole family worshiping together, even though it may be a little disruptive

    or

    b. think that arrangements ought to be made to care for the children in ways that won't intrude on or disrupt the service?

44. If your church was burned down, and you were building a new one (ignoring issues about insurance), would you
    a. hope to incorporate as much of the old building and artifacts as possible

    or

    b. try to create something completely different, abandoning anything from the old building which was still available?

45. Do you think Christian faith is primarily concerned with
    a. transforming the world

    or

    b. transforming my soul?

46. Which of these options most clearly describes you?
    a. You notice little things like whether the surplices are washed and ironed, whether the candles are lit, and whether the church has been cleaned properly

    or

    b. These things tend to pass you by until your attention is drawn to them

47. Are you primarily
    a. appreciative of the local church and its ministry

    or

    b. critical of the local church and its ministry?

48. Which of these pairs do you think is the more important when thinking about the church
    a. structure and tradition

    or

b. flexibility and spontaneity?

49. A good approach to spirituality is one which addresses the subject in
    a. considerable breadth
       or
    b. considerable depth?

50. Do you tend to appreciate a sermon primarily
    a. for the way in which it is crafted, for the way in which it hangs together and the theme develops
       or
    b. for its inspirational qualities and for the vividness of its imagery?

51. Which image of the church do you prefer—that it is a
    a. pastoral community
       or
    b. prophetic community?

52. When doing various pieces of work, do you tend to
    a. be well-organized and prepared
       or
    b. leave things very much to the last minute?

53. Which of these statements describes best how your faith is developed—
    a. having the opportunity to talk it through with others
       or
    b. having the time and space to think by yourself?

54. Which describes you best?
    a. You learn by taking things one step at a time and gradually building up a big picture
       or
    b. You learn by grasping the big picture and then begin to work at the details

55. All these things are important in the life of the church, but would you prefer to be involved in

    a. visiting the sick or bereaved

        or

    b. working on the finance, fabric, and long-term planning issues?

56. Which of these statements is closest to what you think?

    a. When people have questions about life and their experiences the church should be able to give the right answers to them

        or

    b. When people have these sorts of questions, the church needs to be able to understand why they are asking them, and "stand alongside" the questioner in their search for answers

57. Do you think it is more likely that

    a. people begin to think about spiritual things and then seek out a church

        or

    b. people become associated with a church for many reasons and may then begin to think about spiritual matters?

58. When thinking about your church are you primarily concerned about

    a. things as they are, and how they have reached this stage—that is, the present as a continuation of the past

        or

    b. things as they might be, with little reference to the past?

59. Which of these phrases most closely fits your viewpoint

    a. Jesus is my Savior, and therefore, by extension, the Savior of the whole world

        or

    b. Jesus is the Savior of the whole world, and therefore he must also be my Savior?

60. Do you think that the Christian faith offers you, in essence,

> **a.** assurance, security, and structure
>
> or
>
> **b.** adventure, unpredictability, and insecurity?

ANSWER GRID FOR THE QUESTIONNAIRE

Place a check mark in either box **a** or box **b.** NOT IN BOTH!

No.	a	b	No.	a	b	No.	a	b	No.	a	b
1			2			3			4		
5			6			7			8		
9			10			11			12		
13			14			15			16		
17			18			19			20		
21			22			23			24		
25			26			27			28		
29			30			31			32		
33			34			35			36		
37			38			39			40		
41			42			43			44		
45			46			47			48		
49			50			51			52		
53			54			55			56		
57			58			59			60		
Total	1	2	Total	3	4	Total	5	6	Total	7	8

When all the questions have been answered and the numbers placed in the "total boxes" and *not before,* transfer the numbers to the chart on page 117.

4
Spirituality and Personality
Sensing, iNtuition, Feeling, and Thinking

W hen Jesus was asked which of the commandments was the most important he replied,

The most important one is this, "Listen, Israel! The Lord our God is the only Lord. Love the Lord your God with all your heart, with all your soul, with all your mind, and with all your strength." The second most important commandment is this: "Love your neighbor as you love yourself." There is no other commandment more important than these two.[1]

Such an answer makes it quite clear that all of our personality—mind, will, and strength—has to be included in any response that we make to God. We are to be totally involved in such a process. Not only do our love and commitment need to be focused upon God, but also they have to spread out to include others.

There are difficulties, therefore, in trying to single out particular personality functions and explore what effect they have upon our spiritual journey. Such an exercise can only be done with considerable care acknowledging that, in practice, such particularization is virtually impossible. In terms of the Myers-Briggs framework, all personality functions are important. All are present in our spiritual life, and we ignore any of them to our detriment. But just as in our normal day-to-day living our dominant and auxiliary functions tend to mold and shape our personalities in a particular way, so too in our spiritual life they wield their influence. This is especially true when we look at the effects of our third and fourth preferences (our inferior functions or our shadow).

For the moment, though, we need to be able to recognize how different functions manifest themselves in spirituality. The insights offered by Myers Briggs can be of real help in understanding how we relate to different spiritual traditions and patterns of spirituality. I have certainly benefited from them, but they are only a tool. As Lloyd Edwards reminds us:

> . . . neither psychology nor any other modern science can ever
> be an adequate method or provide an adequate language for
> spiritual phenomena. Typology is quite inadequate to describe
> the richness and nuance of spiritual experience. Especially to
> be avoided are tables or charts that claim to correlate type with
> experience, belief or practice—another Procrustean bed that
> psychology offers to spirituality![2]

Having noted that warning let us imagine that we are using a filter to isolate the different influences. A filter has the effect of only letting part of the light through a lens. It soaks up or blocks out those elements which it does not want to use. They are still there, but the effect of the filter is to allow us to concentrate solely on the part that we want. So with personality and prayer, and with spirituality in general, all the functions and parts of our personality are present, all of the time. For convenience we will block out most of them as we turn our attention to the effects and influences of particular functions and processes, namely Sensing, iNtuition, Feeling, and Thinking.

Enjoying the Here and Now . . .

Aspects of Sensing *spirituality*

> Let your soul speak for itself. Some souls hold conversation
> with God in music, and some in the sowing of seed, and others
> in the smell of sawed wood, and still others in the affectionate
> understanding of their friends.[3]

> (Samuel Miller)

Spirituality and Personality

Something like three-quarters of the population are thought to be people whose preference is for Sensing rather than for INtuition, but in the workshops that I have run for church groups it is very rare indeed to find more Sensers than iNtuitives. That in itself presents the church with quite an interesting problem. If the churches attract more iNtuitives than Sensers, as seems to be likely, then it probably means that when people whose preference is for sensing do come to churches they are likely to find a pattern of spirituality more directed to and influenced by iNtuitives. This fact was commented on in Bruce Duncan's interesting book Pray Your Way. He quoted an article in The Daily Telegraph which accused church leaders of underestimating "the importance that simple but readily comprehensible images play in reducing great religious mysteries to concepts which ordinary mortals can come to terms with." But most religious leaders, says Duncan, are recruited from people whose preference is for iNtuition rather than Sensing, and

> their religious symbols are intellectual, conceptual, abstract and philosophical. They dislike any attempt to simplify complexities and mysteries. Not only for their own sakes but for the sake of those they lead and influence, they have an obligation to open themselves to the childlike simplicity and humility of (sensing) prayer.[4]

So what are the characteristics of this approach? Sensers are people who take in information through their senses. Their awareness of the world, and of the spiritual dimension to life comes from their sight, from visual stimuli; from their hearing, so music, speaking, and silence are important to them; and from touch, and smell, and taste. Sensers tend to be concerned with specifics and with the "here and now." "Don't talk of love, show me!" said Eliza Doolittle in the musical My Fair Lady. So in the spiritual realm, Sensers are concerned with what is happening today, here and now, and they are less happy concerning themselves with what they perceive as being vague, generalized plans about the future. If Christianity is to be relevant, it has to be relevant now, to the circumstances in which I find myself, and there must be something practical issuing from it. In essence, the Sensing approach to spirituality is simple: cut out all the complexities, don't baffle me with words and ideas, just let me know in the simplest of terms what it is all about. Surely, they reason, God is near and is loving, and so we must rediscover the simple childlike trust which allows us to enjoy that closeness, and we must beware of making what is essentially simple seem complex and off-putting to people who are not necessarily learned or sophisticated.

I know of one iNtuitive preacher who admits that his heart sinks when, after a sermon, someone asks him what they can do! He enjoys exploring the nature of faith but spends too little time reflecting on its day-to-day implications. A member of one congregation responded to a sermon by volunteering to paint the church toilets; on questioning he declared quite bluntly, "I didn't do it for the Rector: I did it for God." This is the spirituality of a Senser.

For this type of person there are so many things which, day by day, can open doors to God. A summer's day, the beauty of cloud formations, the delicacy of a flower, the smell of newly cut grass, the sounds of the birds or the lapping of the waves on the beach. There is a story about a farmer who was a Methodist local preacher, and at every service his prayers would be full of thanksgiving about the weather. He could always find something of God in the wind, or the cold, the sunshine, or the frost. After one particularly horrendous spell of rain which made farming well nigh impossible, he began his prayers with the words "We thank thee Lord that thou doesn't very often send us weather like this"! Everything can be a reminder of God!

Brian Keenan, in his book An Evil Cradling, describing his time as a hostage in the Middle East, has a very vivid passage illustrating a sensing experience. No doubt his physical and emotional deprivation at the time had a part to play in the intensity of the experience. In the book, just before this passage there is a graphic description of his struggle to find some way of praying:

But wait. My eyes are almost burned by what I see. There's a bowl in front of me that wasn't there before. A brown button bowl and in it some apricots, some small oranges, some nuts, cherries, a banana. The fruits, the colours, mesmerize me in a quiet rapture that spins through my head. I am entranced by colour. I lift an orange into the flat filthy palm of my hand and feel and smell and lick it. The colour orange, the colour, the colour, My God the colour orange. Before me is a feast of colour. I feel myself begin to dance, slowly, I am intoxicated by colour. I feel the colour in a quiet somnambulant rage. Such wonder, such absolute wonder in such an insignificant fruit.

I cannot, I will not eat this fruit. I sit in quiet joy, so complete, beyond the meaning of joy. My soul finds its own completeness in that bowl of colour. The forms of each fruit. The shape and curl and bend all so rich, so perfect. I want to bow before it, loving that blazing, roaring, orange colour . . . Everything meeting in a moment of colour and of form, my rapture no longer an abstract euphoria. It is there in that tiny bowl, the world recreated in that broken bowl.[5]

One of my favorite records is of a concert given by Cleo Laine in the Carnegie Hall in New York some twenty years ago, and I never fail to be moved by the song "You've got to stop, and smell the roses." In it she reflects on the busyness of so many people, and she notes how they rush around and fail to notice so much that is good. Why don't you stop, in the midst of all that busyness, the song says, and go over and take a deep breath by the roses and then you will discover what life is really about. Other songs which come to mind and speak to me of God through my senses are "Starry Starry Night," the song about Vincent van Gogh; "The Streets of London"; and the one about the painter Lowry with words about "matchstick men and women." Perhaps listening to the words of songs, and often being affected by their tunes, is a very common way into spirituality for Sensers.

Many Sensers are aware of their body, in ways which people who prefer the intuitive process find difficult to understand. Attention to the body and breathing can therefore readily find a place in spirituality for Sensers. Deep breathing, being still, becoming "aware" of your body, from the tips of your fingers to the end of your toes are examples of this. An exercise which I have seen used several times, designed to help people become aware of their body and its relationship to the environment, is to ask people to walk around without any shoes on and to feel the ground beneath them. They are encouraged to feel the walls, the doors, and become more aware of the different textures. An exercise like this can be a sheer delight to some people and incredibly difficult for others.

The experience of sensing when applied to church life is graphically described at the beginning of one of Vincent Donovan's books:

> The Catholic church of yesterday had a texture to it, a feel: the smudge of ashes on your forehead on Ash Wednesday, the cool candle against your throat on St. Blaise's day, the waferlike sensation on your tongue in Communion. It had a look; the oddly elegant sight of the silky vestments on the back of the priest as he went about his mysterious rites facing the sanctuary wall in the parish church; the monstrance with its solar radial brilliance surrounding the stark white host of the tabernacle; the indelible impression of the blue-and-white Virgin and the shocking red of the Sacred Heart. It even had a smell, an odor: the pungent incense, the extinguished candles with their beeswax aroma floating ceilingward and filling your nostrils, the smell of olive oil and sacramental balm. It had the taste of fish on Friday and unleavened bread and hot cross buns. It had the sound of unearthly Gregorian chant and flectamus genua and mournful Dies Irae. The church had a way of capturing all your senses, keeping your senses and being enthralled.[6]

When reading the Bible, Sensers are more likely to want to pay attention to specific details, and perhaps to work systematically through a particular book or Gospel. It is often said that they are more attracted to Mark than to the other Gospels because of the way in which the material is handled—quite concisely and specifically and orderly—although I have to confess to being rather skeptical about the idea that different Gospels appeal to different personality types! It is certainly true, however, that most Sensers want things to be clear, uncomplicated, and rooted in reality. That is not to suggest that they are not able to handle complexity, nor to suggest that somehow they are less intelligent. Far from it. We are merely saying that although Sensers can operate using all functions, their preference is for Sensing; and the characteristics of Sensing are immediacy, simplicity, relevance, being approached by and through the senses.

People whose dominant function is Sensing may be Extrovert or Introvert. Introverted Sensers (ISTJ and ISFJ) probably "see" things considerably colored by subjective elements. Their attention is likely to be very selective, guided by their inner interests, and making it much more difficult for others to predict what external stimuli may catch and hold their attention. They may develop what appears to others to be a rather eccentric and individual inner self, seeing things which others do not. Extroverted Sensers on the other hand (ESTP and ESFP) tend to "see" things more as they actually are, and their attention is often grasped by the strongest stimulus which then becomes the center of their attention. They often develop a pleasure-loving outer self, seeking to gratify their senses and thirst for experiences. They may delight in outdoor pursuits, or in facts, knowledge, and concrete realities.

Sensers are often characterized by their sense of stability and contentment. They seem able to enjoy the here and now, and are content to get on with whatever needs doing. This approach influences their devotional life. They prefer a straightforward acceptance of things and a commitment to get on with the job—whether it be prayer or social action or study—rather than making endless plans, or exploring a whole host of alternative possibilities (although if the person is also a Thinker and a Perceiver this may not be quite so pronounced).

Many of our hymns appeal specifically to people with a Sensing preference. Note the practicality, rootedness, and reference to the senses in the following examples:

Teach me my God and king,
in all things thee to see;
and what I do in anything
to do it as for thee.

Knowing Me, Knowing God

A servant with this clause
makes drudgery divine;
who sweeps a room, as for thy laws,
makes that and the action fine.

>All creatures of our God and king
>lift up your voice and with us sing,
>alleluia, alleluia.
>Thou burning sun with golden beam,
>thou silver moon with softer gleam,
>Oh praise him . . .

>Thou rushing wind that art so strong,
>ye clouds that sail in heaven along,
>alleluia, alleluia.
>Thou rising morn, in praise rejoice,
>ye lights of evening, find a voice . . .

Verse two of "Come Down O Love Divine":

Oh let it freely burn,
till earthly passions turn
to dust and ashes in its heat consuming;
and let thy glorious light
shine ever on my sight,
and clothe me round, the while my path
illuming.

Another hymn full of sensate imagery is "Eternal Father, Strong to Save," with the verse that reads:

O Christ whose voice the waters heard
and hushed their raging at thy word,
and walkedst on the foaming deep,
and calm amid the storm didst sleep,
Oh hear us when we cry to thee
for those in peril on the sea.

There are many other examples, from "In the Bleak Mid-winter" with its graphic descriptions of cold and hardness to "All Things

Spirituality and Personality

Bright and Beautiful" with its warm encompassing of the countryside. It is important to remember that the functions of Sensing
or iNtuition, Thinking or Feeling do not occur in isolation; they
all coexist together and we are merely highlighting what are the
dominant processes. Similarly, in hymns there are invariably several emphases, and in picking out one or two to illustrate each
function we must also be conscious of the fact that other factors
are also present in them; they are not wholly and exclusively illustrative of one particular preference. However, it is an interesting
exercise to look through the hymnbook and to try and divide the
hymns into "type appropriate" verses!

Excited by the Big Picture . . .

Aspects of iNtuitive *spirituality*

O God of many colors,
you are like a weaver in our lives.
　　Out of the energy of the universe
　　you have spun each one of us
　　into a unique, colorful strand
　　with our own special hue and texture
　　and have woven us together
　　into your human family
　　that blankets the globe.
Many times our choices
have severed us from your loom of life
　　and created rents in the whole
　　of our human fabric.
　　Our earth is scarred.
　　Your people are aching.
　　We need to weave new tapestries.
O Weaver God,
open our eyes to the mystery and power of your Spirit.
　　Refresh us with the light of your vision
　　so that we may once again recognize
　　the beauty and wonder
　　of the specially spun strands

that we are
and the splendor of the one colorful
cloth of humanity.
Reattach us to your loom
so that your vision may radiate
through us.
O God of many colors and designs,
together let us weave threads into clothing
to warm our old people.
Together let us weave vines into shelter
to house our homeless women, men and children.
Together let us weave friends into families
that offer healing love to our sisters
and brothers hurting from violence.
Together let us weave prayers into actions to heal our
scarred earth.
Amen. Blessed Be. Let it be so.[7]

People whose preference is for iNtuition take in information through their imagination. They tend to be future-oriented, aware of possibilities, and to live in a provisional world. They look for, and hope for, a new and better situation. These preferences are formative in their spiritual life, and shape and mold their approach to worship and prayer as well as their general thinking about God and the world. INtuitives tend to be concerned with the "big picture." They are less concerned about details, and can quickly become bored with repetition, practicalities, and the minutiae of plans and present circumstances. They are therefore attracted to a theology which places stress on the reign of God,[8] a reign which God is bringing about in the world and which will reflect the characteristics of God—justice, peace, the breaking down of barriers, and the holding together of the disparate parts of creation. INtuitives have a transcendent view of God, and like to allow their minds to wander and conceive of new possibilities. To iNtuitives God is so mysterious and wonderful that to use words to describe God—the ultimately unknowable—is to deny God's reality, or at least so to limit what they mean by God that the words become almost meaningless.

Spirituality and Personality

People preferring iNtuition seek to transform the world, and so they are seldom satisfied. They tend to be forever looking for "better" ways of exploring what it means to be a disciple. There is a divine discontent about them, which can be challenging and endearing, but also at times infuriating because of their seeming need to challenge and change everything. One iNtuitive clergyperson was referred to in this way—"I love him dearly, but I do think that every morning he wakes up, looks at himself in the mirror while shaving, and asks himself 'Now what can I change today?' "

INtuitives often like to think about several things at the same time, and so their praying tends to lack focus when compared to that of the Senser. It is as though, when the iNtuitive eventually gets down to prayer (they do not like routine and so there is unlikely to be a set pattern!) and begins to think about the content of their prayer, almost too many possibilities come to mind and they are reluctant to let go of any of them. They like to reflect upon the future and are stimulated and challenged by the many possibilities which are opened up to them. Insatiably curious, they tend to want to ask questions about everything and everyone. So few things can be taken on face value and almost everything can lead to other possibilities. There is a danger that they fail to act because they are so interested in thinking about the alternatives and possibilities! This is particularly true of those iNtuitives who are also Perceivers (with a P as the last letter in their personality profile). Jung himself warned of the danger that extroverted iNtuitives can find themselves facing when he wrote that

> he fritters his life away on things and people, spreading about
> him an abundance of life which others live and not he himself.
> In the end he goes away empty.[9]

INtuitives are likely to pray in generalizations rather than specifics, and when they do focus on a specific, it is likely, very quickly, to turn into a more general prayer. A request to pray for a child in the hospital may lead on to a prayer for all children in hospitals, for all children in need, particularly those in situations

Knowing Me, Knowing God

of danger, in the latest war zone which is in the news . . . and from there the prayer may turn into a prayer for peace so that all children might be able to live without fear and pain and suffering.

INtuitives may be inclined to believe that they get as much insight into the workings of God by reading novels as they do from reading the Bible, and although Scripture may be very important to them, it is likely to be used as a launching-off point for reflective thought about a whole range of issues. It is not so much the specific biblical narrative which is important, as the fact that God may use that Bible passage to bring other things to mind. In public worship iNtuitives may complement scriptural readings with other readings. The other readings may even supplant Scripture; I have been at several weddings where readings from Kahlil Gibran's The Prophet have taken the place of biblical readings, and the following newspaper passage was used as the central reading in a section of a Good Friday service a few years ago to lead people into reflecting on the cry of Jesus "My God, my God, why hast thou forsaken me":

Keya, 18, grieves by the body of her brother-in-law, one of several dead children found in a flooded paddy field after the latest cyclone to hit southwest Bangladesh. Keya has also lost her only son in the disaster—"my mother took him to her village. It has vanished now. O God, tell me where my son is. Is he alive or dead?" she asked foreign aid workers who reached her ruined village . . . the official death toll is just short of 2,000, but more than 12,000 people, many of them fishermen, are missing and the final death toll could reach 10,000.

Keya tells of the rain being followed by strong winds and a tidal wave. "We were praying. The wind started blowing stronger. My husband came and held me tightly. At the same time I felt a hot air with tremendous speed take away our roof. I cried out in fear and asked God for mercy. We heard people screaming and children crying." Their adobe house was destroyed, and their barn and two-month supply of grain was washed away. Their livestock was killed and crops ruined. Other survivors are still looking for missing children. Dead animals, upturned boats, and the broken frames of houses float in sur-

Spirituality and Personality

rounding streams or are tangled in the branches of mangrove trees. The victims need food, clothing, and housing. But aid workers say that most importantly, they need to prepare for a new harvest in order to be able to feed themselves and end their dependence on foreign aid.[10]

Why has thou forsaken me, indeed? The person who prefers iNtuition is likely to find that reflecting on a passage such as that complements and draws out the meaning of the passion stories in the Gospels. In fact iNtuitives may want to go further and argue that unless and until the Gospel stories are brought home to us in contemporary situations such as that, then they are actually failing to engage us in an authentic way.

INtuitive Thinkers (INTP, INTJ, ENTP, and ENTJ) often find that their devotional life is enhanced by theological questioning, and they look to develop a spirituality which draws upon reason as a basis for thought and reflection. INtuitive Feelers (INFP, INFJ, ENFP, and ENFJ), however, like a spirituality which involves and values the whole person. INtuitives often work in bursts of enthusiasm followed by lean periods, and the same can be true of their spirituality. There can be periods of intense insight, devotion, or activity followed by lulls, which may be of indeterminate length. The mature iNtuitive has learned not to be unduly worried by these times of barrenness. Like anyone else, of course, the iNtuitive can become self-indulgent, fickle, or just plain difficult! There may be occasions when, for a whole variety of reasons, he or she does not pay sufficient attention to the important things in life, and consequently they may find that their spiritual development suffers. That happens not because they are iNtuitives but because they are human! Being an iNtuitive, however, they may also have barren patches which are specifically related to their personality type. A certain degree of perception is required to be able to distinguish one type of barrenness from the other.

Extroverted iNtuitives may be concerned with the possibilities of making considerable changes to the external environment, and with searching the worlds of ideas and events for new possibilities. They are always looking for new ways of understanding and cooperating with God. Introverted iNtuitives, on the other hand, might have less concern for making changes "out there," and be more interested in revising their way of looking at things, and searching out new angles for understanding life. Introverted iNtuitive prayer can be very deep and people who have mastered this form of prayer are often respected as spiritual writers or teachers. INtuitives live in a provisional world, full of exciting possibilities, and they tend to see things on a grand scale. The salvation of the world is more appealing than the salvation of a single soul! Added to this, they are curious and always asking questions, as this example shows:

> Our particular culture poses the question of how the gospel message can be heard. Our responsibility through worship and faith to be under the revelation of the gospel poses the question of what things should be heard. So, for example, within the confused, pluralistic and in many ways post-Christian culture of my country the gospel issue is necessarily much more in terms of "are God and his kingdom a possibility?" than "is Jesus our Savior"?[11]

John's Gospel is said to appeal to iNtuitives, with its rich imagery and symbolism. It is quite difficult finding hymns which clearly stress an iNtuitive approach, but among those that might be considered is:

> I danced in the morning when the world was begun
> And I danced in the moon and the stars and the sun,
> And I came down from heaven and I danced on the
>   earth;
> At Bethlehem I had my birth.
>
> Dance then, wherever you may be;
> I am the Lord of the Dance, said he,
> And I'll lead you all, wherever you may be,
> And I'll lead you all in the dance, said he.

Spirituality and Personality

They cut me down and I leap up high;
I am the life that'll never, never die;
I'll live in you if you'll live in me
I am the Lord of the Dance, said he.
    Dance then . . .

Taken from LORD OF THE DANCE by Sydney Carter © 1963 by Stainer & Bell Ltd. Used by permission of Hope Publishing Co., Carol Stream, IL 60188. All rights reserved. Used by permission.

The idea of a cosmic Christ is very appealing to iNtuitives, but the person who is struggling to come to terms with their feelings of anger against their next-door neighbor, their mother or son, and who is confused as to what an appropriate Christian response is, might be less than excited by a hymn which tries to work out whether, if there is life on Mars, there would need to be a Martian incarnation, as suggested in these verses from Sidney Carter's lovely iNtuitive hymn "Every Star Shall Sing a Carol":

> Who can tell what other cradle
> high above the milky way
> still may rock the King of Heaven
> on another Christmas Day?
>
> Who can count how many crosses
> still to come or long ago
> crucify the King of Heaven?
> holy is the name I know.

Taken from EVERY STAR SHALL SING A CAROL by Sydney Carter © 1961, 1974 by Stainer & Bell Ltd. Used by permission of Hope Publishing Co., Carol Stream, IL 60188. All rights reserved. Used by permission.

An iNtuitive's creed might be one like this:
    We believe in God,
    whose love is the source of all life
        and the desire of our lives.
    Whose love was given a human face
        in Jesus of Nazareth.
    Whose love was crucified by the evil
        that waits to enslave us all,
    and whose love, defeating even death

Knowing Me, Knowing God

is our glorious promise of freedom.
Therefore, though we are sometimes fearful
    and full of doubt,
    in God we trust;
and in the name of Jesus Christ, we commit ourselves,
    in the service of others,
    to seek justice,
    and to live in peace,
    to care for the earth and to share
        the commonwealth of God's goodness.
    To live in the freedom of forgiveness,
        and in the power of the spirit of love,
    And in the company of the faithful
        so to be the church.
    For the Glory of God. Amen.[12]

A creed such as this may be seen as being an improvement on, or more appropriate than the traditional creed. Some people will respond to it with enthusiasm, and it will open up new ideas or fresh possibilities, while others may well wonder what has been gained and what a lot has been lost! Once again, it is important to remember that most church leaders are probably iNtuitives, and most people in the population are probably Sensers.

I have spent some considerable time on this Sensing-iNtuitition dimension because I think it is of profound importance in our churches today. Much contemporary debate and division in theology is, to my mind, not so much about theology as about personality. Take, for instance, the incident in Mark (4:35-41) where Jesus is asleep in a boat when a storm erupts, frightening the disciples who are with him. The scene is quite clear for the Senser. The biblical text is straightforward, and he or she can imagine the scene and identify with it. Jesus quells the storm in a miraculous way, and it is another concrete example of his power, and a sign of his divinity. For an iNtuitive, it is much more difficult to take an isolated incident like this and to make deductions from it. It needs to be part of an overall pattern, in the iNtuitive's eyes, and has to be seen in a much larger context. To speak of the quelling of a particular storm does not necessarily suggest the power of God—in fact it can be seen to

70

diminish and reduce the amazing, mysterious, and all-powerful God. It is difficult for the iNtuitive to be excited by a specific example. But when iNtuitives reflect on the fact that very often in the ancient world water represented chaos, they may come to the conclusion that this story symbolically recounts how Jesus was able to quell the powers of chaos. It then takes on a new meaning and an important significance. Both the Senser and the iNtuitive see a miracle. For both of them the story is about God's power made manifest in Jesus, but their different ways of handling the story could lead to arguments and division within the church. One could be accused of simplistic literalism and the other of denying the truth of Scripture.

Being Involved Yourself . . .

Aspects of Feeling *spirituality*

> It is a lavishing of precious resources, our precious ointment on the handicapped, the insane, the rejected and the dying that most clearly reveals the love of Christ in our times. It is this gratuitous caring, this unilateral declaration of love which proclaims the gospel more powerfully than bishops and theologians . . . More than anything I have discovered that the world is not divided into the sick and those who care for them, but that we are all wounded and that we all contain within our hearts that love which is for the healing of the nations.[13]
> (Sheila Cassidy)

The Feeling function is one which is concerned with Judgment, with determining how we use all the material we have obtained through our Perceiving functions. It is concerned with making judgments and decisions based upon values. A person who prefers their Feeling function—we are using the word here in a technical sense and not implying that people who are Thinkers do not feel—nor that people who prefer their Feeling function do not think—is one who is particularly concerned about the effect that a decision or an action will have upon the other people involved. It is probable that there are far more people of this sort in our churches than any other. It is thought that about sixty percent of all women prefer their Feeling function and about forty percent of all men, but a far higher proportion than this, of both sexes, attend the workshops I run for church groups. It is still too early to have reliable statistics but figures suggest that overall Feelers outnumber Thinkers in the church by approximately three to one.

Those who prefer Feeling will tend to think that decisions are good if they take other people into account, and they will put themselves out for the sake of others. They will tend to place themselves in other people's shoes and will enjoy helping others. They prize peace and harmony and go to considerable lengths to create such conditions, often at personal expense or inconvenience. They also often turn a blind eye to things which ought to be challenged or to people who need to be confronted.

It is very easy for Feeling types to identify with gospel images and situations. They easily drop into the role of sacrificial victim, the person who turns the other cheek or goes the extra mile, and they often see positive merit in bearing the suffering of others. It is almost as though it is more Christlike to be hurt. There can sometimes be an unconscious desire to be exploited or "put upon," for that can be interpreted as a sign of authentic discipleship. Were we not warned that there would be a price to pay and that the road was not easy? Generations of Christians have been brought up on images of suffering love which might have more to do with the Feeling preference than with authentic discipleship.

The spirituality of the Feeler recognizes that the heart has reasons which the mind may not be able to comprehend. There is a built-in suspicion of what the Feeler interprets as too cerebral an approach to faith. The personal, subjective, and intimate approach is preferred, and this focuses upon a personal relationship with God. This is at the heart of things. As St. Augustine said, "You have made us for yourself and our heart is restless till it finds its rest in You."

People who prefer the Feeling function are often rather vul-

Spirituality and Personality

nerable. They can take on themselves the blame for any situation which lacks harmony, or which fails to fulfill its potential. They find it hard to worship in situations where there is not a basic peace and harmony, and have a tendency to suppress their own wants and needs in order to comply with what they think other people may be wanting. This "super-sensitivity" can be quite a burden for them to carry sometimes, but it often allows them to have an instinctive "feel" for a congregation and therefore to be sympathetic and sensitive leaders of worship. They will tend to know how long a silence should last, and for how long people can usefully and creatively handle it.

Feelers' understanding of God is personal, and from their own experience they know that God is compassionate and forgiving, loving and very near. God's capacity for loving acceptance is infinite. Female imagery may spring to mind: the mother hen guarding her chicks; as a mother loves her children so does God remain loving and faithful; as childbirth is both painful and joyful so are God's creative endeavors in the world today.

A prayer which speaks straight to the heart of the Feeling person comes in the Order for a Communion Service written by William Barclay:

Come, not because you are strong, but because you are
　weak.
Come, not because any goodness of your own gives you a
　right to come, but because you need mercy and help.
Come, because you love the Lord a little and would like
　to love him more.
Come, because he loved you and gave himself for you.
Lift up your hearts and minds above your cares and fears
　and let this bread and wine be to you the token and
　pledge of the grace of the Lord Jesus Christ, the love
　of God and the fellowship of the Spirit, all meant for
　you if you will receive them in humble faith.
I will take the cup of salvation and call upon the Lord.
Blessed are they who hunger and thirst after righteous-
　ness for they shall be filled.
Oh taste and see that God is good.[14]

To Feelers, commitment to a church community is important. It is the focal point for spiritual growth, for getting to know people, discovering their needs and their troubles, and providing strength, succor, and understanding for themselves. The church is seen as being a welcoming, serving community, which is there to encourage and sustain its members and to offer a hand of friendship to those who are not its members. One image of the church was given by a woman who had been seriously ill and felt that she had been wonderfully sustained by the praying community. "I have been carried along on a surfboard of love" she said, and all who knew her knew exactly what she meant.

People who have the Feeling function as their dominant and are also Extroverts (ESFJ, ENFJ) may find that their behavior is greatly influenced by external factors, by the situations in which they find themselves, or by the people that they are with. They will tend to find expressing themselves and sharing with others relatively easy, and their goal is the formation and maintaining of harmonious and friendly relationships with other people. Their network of contacts may be extensive although not necessarily very deep. They may like to pray in the company of others, and be committed to a whole range of practical acts of service. People who prefer Feeling who are also Introverts (ISFP, INFP) may find that their behavior is influenced mainly by internal factors, by their strong sense of values which leads them to act accordingly, and that it is prompted less by the external situation in which they find themselves. Their relationships may be deep, passionate even, rather than extensive; and their goal is the fostering and protection of an inner emotional life which is at peace. Their inner feelings may sometimes be so strong that they cannot adequately be expressed and so they may give the impression of being rather cool or even indifferent when actually the opposite may well be the case. Introverted Feeling types may spend a great deal of time in private intercessory prayer, thus combining their concern for people in their specific situations with their need for solitude and depth.

In their personal devotional life Introverted Feelers may be helped by keeping a diary or a spiritual log book in which they record their thoughts and reflections at regular times. There are several ways of doing this, but one is to write thoughts down on one page of a book or diary, leaving the opposite page blank, for yourself only to read, date it, and then perhaps three, six, or twelve months later reread what you were concerned about at that time and perhaps make notes on the opposite blank page—remembering to date the entry. In this way, over the months and years it is possible to build up a record of "conversations with God," causes for thanksgiving, and opportunities for praise. They may also want to keep a record of their dreams, again for personal reflection only.

People with a Feeling preference who have iNtuition as a dominant or auxiliary (INFP, INFJ, ENFP, ENFJ) are often attracted to a spirituality that operates on a broad canvas, that looks for universal values and possibilities; while those who have Sensing as a dominant or auxiliary (ISFP, ISFJ, ESFP, ESFJ) may be committed to practical acts of social care—prison visiting, meals on wheels, hospital duty, work with the homeless, or maintaining an "open house" with time to listen to people and care for them.

Few people can doubt the authenticity of a Feeling person's understanding of God. They may want to add a little more to it, but the emphasis upon love and acceptance, upon forgiveness and reconciliation is seen to lie at the heart of our faith. These characteristics also feature prominently in Luke's Gospel—said to be favored by Feelers—and they are expressed in a great many of our hymns.

The God of love my shepherd is,
  and he that doth me feed;
while he is mine and I am his,
  what can I want or need?

      Make me a channel of your peace.
      Where there is hatred, let me bring your
        love;
      Where there is injury your pardon, Lord;
      And where there's doubt, true faith in
        you . . .

Knowing Me, Knowing God

O Master, grant that I may never seek
So much to be consoled as to console;
To be understood as to understand;
To be loved, as to love with all my soul.

"Dear Lord and Father of Mankind," "O Jesus I Have Promised," "And Can It Be," "Love Divine All Loves Excelling" . . . the list is almost endless, each hymn focusing upon the love of God and the way in which that love can enter our own lives and transform our being so that we become fellow-workers with God in establishing harmony, reconciliation, and peace in a broken and sinful world.

Hanging on to Integrity . . .

Aspects of Thinking spirituality

> We can never approach a Christian theology of other religions as though there is anywhere a possibility of getting beyond dispute; there is only the way of disputing creatively and recreatively rather than destructively.[15]
>
> (Haddon Willmer)

The above quotation illustrates what is at the heart of a Thinking approach to spirituality. Again, "Thinking" is used in a technical sense and is not meant to imply that those who prefer the Feeling function are non-thinkers. God is perceived as being primarily righteous, just, faithful, true, consistent, wise, and reasonable (not offending reason). This God created humankind and created us as thinking people, capable of making rational judgments, and therefore God presumably expected us to use our intellects and to offer them as part of our self-offering to God. Thinking spirituality has an element of toughness in it, in that truth is truth and cannot be molded or twisted to suit circumstances or to avoid giving offense. Eric James writes of the anger that he felt at the death of a friend—"Prayer is a kind of questioning—a kind of accusing—of God. There's plenty of that kind of prayer in, for instance, the Psalms: 'O God, wherefore art thou absent from us so long? Why is thy wrath so hot against the sheep of thy pasture?' "[16]

In discussions about theology and other faiths there will, inevitably, be differences of opinion, of outlook, and of fact—as illustrated by the quotation above. They are not to be avoided, and if we are seekers after truth then they are to be confronted, head-on if need be. We can seek to avoid hurt or pain, and probably do and should do, but not if it compromises truth. If we compromise truth then we compromise integrity and without that then our standing as human beings, created in some way in the image of God, crumbles. This is not the same as saying that other faiths are all inadequate, demonic, or anti-God as some people suggest, and that the only stance for Christians is one of conquering evangelism. But it is to say that it helps no one, in the meeting or dialogue with people of other faiths, to assume that we all basically believe the same and therefore we should keep quiet about our areas of difference.

The spirituality of the Thinker tends to be firm, logical, cool, and analytical. It can often be assertive, critical, adversarial, distant, and impersonal. Such a combination can be rather annoying, but our Thinking function does not come isolated from the rest of our personality, and many Thinkers are also people of considerable personal tenderness and care. It is just that their preference is for the Thinking process, and if this is their dominant or auxiliary then it will be shaping their spiritual outlook.

Concepts like being stewards of creation, being responsible and concerned about truth and justice are likely to be part of the Thinker's mindset. God is experienced as making demands upon our lives, requiring us to live with integrity, and to seek righteousness and freedom. It is very much an ethical stance. Prayer is thus seen as a raising of both our hearts and our minds to God, and there will always be a critical commentary running alongside the prayers that are offered. Thinkers like objectivity and exactness, and they like public worship to be done decently and with order. They tend not to like their privacy being invaded, especially if they are also Introverts.

Extroverted dominant Thinkers (ESTJ and ENTJ) concentrate on the external data, with a goal of solving, discovering, modifying, or developing accepted ideas or insights; while Introverted Thinkers concentrate on working on the internal data of belief systems with the goal of creating theories, developing insights, and clarifying an internal framework. Thus, in the realm of spirituality the Extrovert will be pressing forward to ask new questions and explore new areas, while the Introvert will be more interested in developing a scheme or framework of belief, checking out doctrine, and rigorously analyzing new information.

It is important to realize that for Thinkers the very process of thinking can be a form of spiritual exercise. Their capacity and determination to think clearly itself can be an offering to God. They are often more at ease with such a process than with the more self-conscious types of public worship. Thinkers often find such worship a very real problem as, inevitably, they are questioning all the prayers and hymns and checking out their words to see if they are logical, consistent, or true. At a recent conference a most stimulating session urging us to ask basic questions and explore new ideas was almost ruined for me by a worship session being tacked on to the end of it, which took everything for granted and asked no questions. For me, the exploration of ideas was itself an act of worship and what followed was a hollow mockery.

Some forms of worship can be excruciatingly embarrassing for a Thinker, and while they may be happy for others to worship in that way, they really want to have nothing to do with it themselves, and when caught up in such a situation they often really do not know how to handle it. Thus Thinkers very often make a point of staying away from church, because they just do not know how to handle the things which affront their thinking processes. They are not wanting to appear superior or arrogant, but that is often how they appear to others. I recently asked a young woman if she would be attending a particular annual service, and she grimaced and said, slightly embarrassed, "I'm not sure, you see when you start thinking there's really no place for you in church anymore, is there?" She was not wanting to suggest that people in church were mindless or unthinking, but rather, that for her it was no longer possible to maintain her integrity unless she could think about and challenge church worship. She was not opposed to the church, or feeling superior—in fact quite the reverse—but it was just that she could no longer face the inner tension that church attendance brought.

Thinking prayer is often full of doubts and points of view. It can also be angry with God, and believes that this is totally acceptable. It can be highly self-critical and deprecating, but also can be effective, well thought through, consistent, and to the point. On balance, Thinkers tend to regard themselves as rather inadequate when it comes to prayer, and rather left out of things when thoughts turn to spirituality, because they cannot really claim to have had many "spiritual experiences." Such experiences as they might have had they have analyzed time and time again, and have come to some intellectually satisfactory explanation for them. A bishop once told me that in all his life he could only remember having one religious experience and that was hearing Tito Gobi and Maria Callas sing "Tosca" at Covent Garden—and that was something that fed his soul for years and he was quite happy to accept as a "religious experience."

Within our churches, Thinkers tend to be rather few in number and feel themselves marginalized in a culture which is heavily Feeling-biased. It is difficult for men Thinkers; but it is even more difficult for women Thinkers because there are fewer of them and they have to battle with the "female equals Feeling" stereotype that is all too pervasive in our society. Parish ministry tends to be heavily "Feeling influenced," and a great many clergy whose preference is for Thinking rather than Feeling move out, into various sector ministries.

Duncan says of Thinking spirituality:

(It) gazes on the truth . . . it is a rational relationship with God that loves to be stretched to the limits of argument and logic, to follow thoughts to the place where thought runs out. It is opening your mind to the mind of the infinite. It searches for truth and is always asking "Why?" . . . (it) celebrates the gift of knowledge and the ability to meet God with the mind through Scripture and the study of theology.[17]

Thinking spirituality tends to be cerebral and objective, and invariably finds itself being rather defensive, but it has an important role to play in the life of the church. It is essential if the church is to explore and maintain its doctrine and not be swept off course by every passing enthusiasm which comes along. It will never be a popular form of spirituality, and will often be misunderstood and even disparaged, but for people who hold to the Thinking preference it is an essential aspect of their faith. Thinkers are said to prefer Matthew's Gospel with its clear structure, its beginning and end, and its fulfillment of the Law.

Thinking hymns might include "God Be in My Head and in My Understanding." "My Song Is Love Unknown" has a Thinking structure but much Feeling content, and a sense of responsibility and commitment is well expressed in the hymn from Pilgrim's Progress:

> Who would true valor see,
> let him come hither;
> one here will constant be,
> come wind, come weather;
> there's no discouragement
> shall make him once relent
> his first avowed intent
> to be a pilgrim.

In the Breadth and Depth of Life . . .

Aspects of Extrovert *and* Introvert *spirituality*

It is not really possible to deal with Extroversion and Introversion in the same way that we have dealt with the other preferences. They have all been aspects of either Judging or

Spirituality and Personality

Perceiving, but when we look at the Extrovert–Introvert continuum we are considering where and how a person is energized,
enthused, and sustained. It is this preference which seems to be
so important when reflecting upon spirituality, because most
Extroverts find prayer very difficult; and Introverts tend to find
that traditional patterns of prayer and the practices that have
been passed on to them are relatively easy to come to terms
with. (Not easy in the sense that they don't have to struggle at
times, but in the sense that these patterns seem to "fit" their
personality in the way that round pegs fit round holes.)

The Introvert looks for God within; it is an inner journey that
they make. The Extrovert seeks God at work in the world, and is
looking for people who are engaged with the issues of the day.
It is important to remember that everyone can be both Extrovert
and Introvert, and at times they have to choose to operate in
one mode rather than the other, but they will also have a basic
preference for one. That is the preference which is more influential in making them the person that they are. This description of
a "spiritual-minded person" by a fourteenth-century Dominican
is a good example of classic Introverted spirituality:

> [He] should recollect himself in the central point of his soul and
> raise his heart to God with great might, inwardly gazing upon
> God's presence, and ardently longing for whatever is dearest to
> God's will. He should die to self and to all created things and
> immerse himself ever deeper in God's most holy will.[18]

It seems likely that most devotional books are written by
Introverts, and Introverted spirituality tends to be the norm in
our churches. But many of our church members are Extroverts,
and this will mean that for a great many of them they are having to operate in their less-preferred mode. Extroverts will not
feel completely "at home" with what goes on, and they will
have trouble identifying with the prevailing pattern. At the same
time, their own preferences will be largely ignored by clergy
and a tradition steeped in Introvert insights, language, and
experience.

Perhaps a word of encouragement for Extroverts comes

when we turn the emphasis away from individualized private devotions and stress the importance of corporate prayer within the worshiping community. As Eugene Peterson wrote:

> The paradigmatic prayer is not solitary but in community. The fundamental biblical context is worship. That is why worship seems to me to be the place. It's the only context in which we can recover the depth of the gospel. . . . If someone comes to me and says "Teach me how to pray," I say "Be at this church at nine o'clock on Sunday morning." That's where you learn to pray. Of course prayer is continued and has alternate forms when you're by yourself. But the American experience has the order reversed. In the long history of Christian spirituality, community prayer is most important, then individual prayer.[19]

Extroverts often feel that they are unable to pray. This has perhaps been the single most helpful comment that I have come across in my own journey, as an Extrovert, to come to terms with prayer. Perhaps it is that Extroverts cannot pray Introvert prayers with the conviction and integrity that they would like to bring to prayer. Perhaps they need to discover and feel happy in a different sort of prayer, and perhaps the church and clergy need to recognize and honor a different experience and pattern. I have been encouraged by remembering the verse in Ecclesiasticus (38:34):

> . . . . they maintain the fabric of the world
> and their work is their prayer.

A good example of Extroverted spiritual direction comes from Vincent Donovan:

> It is difficult to arrive at the maturity of realizing that the God we pray to will be a silent God, as silent as a winter night or a breathless desert noontime. We get no answer to our prayer. We hear no voice of God. It requires maturity to realize that God does indeed respond to us, does answer us, does speak to us, as God has always done, in that primary locale of revelation—in creation, in the universe, in the world of created human beings that surround us. To grow from childhood, as a

Spirituality and Personality

Christian, we have to look at the world in order to understand God and the sacraments of God, and in order to enter into dialogue with God there.[20]

Introverts will feel as ease shutting themselves off from the world and all its pressures; in fact they may see this as being a prerequisite for prayer. The Extrovert will tend to think that prayer is impossible without wrestling with all these problems. Of all the differences in personality, it is the difference between Extrovert and Introvert which is most significant when exploring prayer.

Living it out in the World . . .

Aspects of Perceiving *and* Judging *spirituality*

It is also difficult to speak of Perceiving and Judging spirituality. These aspects too cannot be handled in quite the same way as the four preferences dealt with earlier. Judging and Perceiving, like Extroversion and Introversion, provide the framework within which the other processes operate. Thinking and Feeling are themselves Judging processes, and everyone has a preference for one or the other; and Sensing and iNtuition are Perceiving processes, and again, everyone has a preference for one or the other.

It is possible to make just one or two general observations, relating to the letter which is at the end of anyone's type description (J or P). People with a P at the end may well reflect upon the fact that they are often open to many different paths, that they try many different routes and can live with a considerable amount of ambiguity. Those with a J at the end of their type description will probably find that they tend to like things to be settled; they dislike living with ambiguity. They may well be drawn to rather more "definite" forms of spirituality, be less open to exploration and, once they have found an appropriate church or congregation, they are likely to develop a considerable loyalty to it and be rather reluctant to see too much change, unless that change is brought about in an orderly and agreed manner. It has been suggested, but I do not have sufficient evidence to substantiate such suggestions, that Js of all people are likely to go off on a false trail and follow a pattern of spirituality least suited to them. This is because, disliking ambiguity, they are likely to want to make a choice quickly and "get on with it"!

5
The Shadow

The accounts of some of the people held hostage by the Shiite Muslims in Beirut during the late 1980s give us vivid accounts of captivity, and examples of truly amazing courage. They also provide us with moving insights into what it means to be human. Brian Keenan writes:

> The act of writing the book was part of a long process of healing which in truth commenced under the most extreme conditions of deprivation and abuse. During my captivity I, like my fellow hostages, was forced to confront the man I thought I was and to discover that I was many people. I had to befriend these many people, discover their origins, introduce them to each other and find a communality between themselves and myself. . . . John and I . . . also discovered a renewed love for the world and its possibilities which, whilst nascent in us as children, had become buried by the accretions of the conscious worlds we had been brought up in.[1]

Immediately on his release, while at the Dutch Embassy in Damascus, he said "I feel like a cross between Humpty Dumpty and Rip Van Winkle—I have fallen off the wall and suddenly awake I find all the pieces of me, before me. There are more parts than I began with!"

Terry Waite's experience was similar although naturally he expresses it in a different way:

> I look back over the years of my captivity. I have had no great

thoughts, no illuminating inspirations. Better men than myself would have been able to dig deeper into their inner experience. All I seem to have done is keep afloat and withstand the storms. . . .

Each day I have walked through the Psalmist's valley. The shadow of death has been around me. Then, for a space, I have caught a glimpse of the warmth of light, and the shadow has receded. Christ in his teaching spoke so simply and yet so profoundly about the essential fundamentals of life.

Who is this mysterious figure who speaks through the pages of the New Testament? My knowledge of him is culturally conditioned. I know that he has taught me to face life as it is and not to be afraid of death. I may die in captivity. I may not see my family and friends again. Whatever happens, I have not been destroyed. My prayers have been puny, but once or twice I have touched the awesome mystery which lies at the heart of the universe, and which I call God. Awesome is the only word I can find to describe what I mean. In Christ I see the light side of God, which gives me strength and hope. His death graphically illustrates the polarity I know in my inner being. By allowing my unconscious to work, I will find healing and strength.[2]

We too can find health and healing, strength and courage if we begin to work with, and on, our unconscious, on what many people call "our shadow." In order to get the best view of a stained-glass window it is necessary to walk into the darkness of a church and look out toward the light. So too it is often necessary for us to explore the inner darknesses of our personality and this can allow the light to illuminate them. In this way we can have a better understanding of ourselves, and develop a spirituality that is honest and attempts to offer to God the totality of our being. This includes not only those parts that we are pleased with and find acceptable, but also those bits of ourselves which we have previously relegated into our subconscious.

Robert Bly speaks of the "long bag we drag behind us"[3] and suggests that it is as though each one of us drags behind us a large, heavy bag. It is invisible, but its effect upon us is extremely powerful. We have put into that bag all the things which we have not been able to cope with during our lives. We began as tiny children recognizing those parts of us which were not acceptable to our parents. These things we repressed; we put them into the bag. School days brought new experiences, new aspects of behavior, that were not acceptable and which we hastily put away in order to gain or retain affection. Each new friendship, each new situation brought the possibilities of adding to the contents of the bag, until at last, we drag a very heavy load. We are not conscious of what we have put away; we have succeeded in forgetting the situations which caused our original anxieties. Just occasionally, when our defenses are down, might the bag spring a leak and that part of us which we choose not to acknowledge bursts out—often causing considerable confusion and embarrassment for us and for others. Sometimes it can be devastating, when we act "completely out of character" and perhaps destroy someone or something in the process. Any part of ourselves that we do not find acceptable is likely to be pushed away, hidden, and can develop the potential to do us harm; just as in the Middle Ages princes or dukes who were banished from the king's court were always a potential focus for revolts or rebellions. Families, groups, institutions, even nations also have their shadows, the things which are never mentioned and which are repressed.

"There is a great deal of unmapped country within us which would have to be taken into account in an explanation of our gusts and storms" wrote George Eliot in Daniel Deronda. Every person has this repressed, unconscious side to them. It is part of being human. I know of workshops on the shadow where, over a period of time, participants literally place heavy objects in a large plastic bag which is tied around their waist. As the workshop progresses so the weight increases, and movement becomes more difficult and hindered. The bag stays with the participants for the whole workshop, at mealtimes, at the toilet, or even in bed. It is a graphic representation of the unconscious load which we each carry around with us. The road to maturity is to learn how to handle it, to come face to face with who we are, and learn how to live with that "other" person.

Knowing Me, Knowing God

William Miller in his book Make Friends with Your Shadow says:

> Substantially more harm is done by denying and repressing the shadow than by coming to grips with it. Those who deny their shadows only project their evil on to others, and see it in them. Those who repress their shadows to maintain their purity and innocence are sometimes overcome by them and swept away in their very own evil. . . . I am not a complete person until I incorporate into my conscious self that dark side of my person which is every bit as much part of me as is that bright side which I parade before the world.[4]

Miller mentions here the important process of projection. This is what happens when we assign to other people those aspects of our own character that we find difficult to accept. An interesting exercise is to ask people to think of someone they know whom they don't like, and invite them to write a list of what it is about that person that brings about the feelings of dislike. Very often what emerges is a list of aspects of our own character that we find difficult to cope with and which we therefore "project" onto someone else. For instance, we might think a colleague is quite a nice person but we dislike his ambitious streak. Upon careful reflection what we might discover is that we find it difficult to accept and cope with our own ambitious desires, so we repress them and pretend that we don't have them. But they are still part of us and they can make their presence felt by influencing our perception of someone else. What it is that we dislike in that person is not their ambition but ours, which we have projected onto them because we have failed to acknowledge it in ourselves. Projection is a self-deceptive process, harming not only the person we have projected onto but also ourselves. The gospel story of seeing a speck of sawdust in someone else's eye while ignoring the plank in our own is an illustration of projection.

It is difficult to arrive at a universally accepted definition of the shadow. It has been described as "the personification of certain aspects of the unconscious personality which could be added to the ego complex but which, for various reasons are not," or "a mythological name for all that is within me which I cannot directly know." Marie-Louise von Franz[5] (who gave those definitions) was a former pupil and collaborator of Jung. She observed that Jung disliked great theories being constructed by people who didn't really have all the knowledge. On one occasion when a student was holding forth he suddenly burst out, "This is all nonsense! The shadow is simply the whole unconscious."

Those who want to understand the Jungian concepts better will need to come to grips with ideas about the conscious, the unconscious, and shadow; the anima and the animus; archetypes and the ego. There are many introductory texts now available.[6] I am particularly interested in exploring here the shadow as it relates to the Myers-Briggs Type Indicator. It is the name which is often given to what are also called the least-preferred, the tertiary and fourth functions, or inferior functions. The very fact that no agreed terminology has been settled on bears witness to this being quite a new area of exploration, and also to the fact that it is all rather imprecise!

In chapter 2 we saw how each person has a dominant and an auxiliary function, which means that each person's personality is strongly influenced by their preferences in two particular areas, and these two interact with each other and support each other. If iNtuition (for example) is the dominant or most influential of the preferences, then it makes sense to argue that the least influential function will be at the other end of the axis from iNtuition (in this example), which is Sensing. That will therefore be the least-preferred, or fourth function. Similarly, if a person's auxiliary function is Thinking (for example) then the opposite end of that axis is Feeling and that will be the person's tertiary function. Thus, the person whose dominant and auxiliary are N and T (which is the case for me) will have least-preferred functions of S and F, and these will be instrumental in forming that person's shadow.

In Myers-Briggs terms, the shadow is seen as being the opposite to the type description which you have for yourself. In my case, being an ENTP, my shadow is then ISFJ. Time and time again it is borne out that people find their "opposites" or shadows the most difficult people to relate to, because they represent all the preferences which have been rejected! Having said that, I must immediately say that that is an over-simplification, and it occasionally happens that people marry their opposite types, seeing in them all the qualities that they do not possess themselves. This was the case for Isabel Briggs Myers herself. However, having made that caveat quite clear, it nevertheless seems to be the case that invariably we find it easier to communicate with, and understand, people who "speak the same language." We very often (although not always) find the functions which we have not preferred quite difficult to handle, and part of the value of the Myers-Briggs Type Indicator is to help us to identify and understand why this should be so, so that we can work on those things which we find difficult and which may be hindering our growth to wholeness.

Just as we find it difficult to write with what is not our normal "writing hand," so we often find it difficult to use our least-preferred functions fluently and appropriately. This is a problem in the ordinary everyday aspects of our life, and it is also a problem in our spiritual life. We usually try to run the spiritual aspects of our life using our preferred functions. That is, we do what comes naturally to us, and what we are best at doing. It makes sense to us to offer the very best that we have to God. We therefore tend to develop our devotional life and our spiritual awareness along the paths that have been well-trodden by the other aspects of our personality. But there are dangers in such an approach, precisely because we are reasonably good at handling it. One commentator put it this way:

> It is precisely in the realm of the inferior function, where the depth of one's commitment to his relationship with God, in humble acceptance of himself and desire for transformation, meets the real test. The religious experience of conversion will always be accompanied in some manner by an eruption of the inferior function as it reveals the individual's state of disintegration, rendering him helpless and in need of the healing of God's love and acceptance in grace.[7]

The Shadow

In our journey to God, we slowly but inevitably become aware of the fact that, when we say that we want to offer our all to God, this must include those parts of our being which we have spent such a long time burying, hiding, ignoring, and denying. Our journey to God really is one of being stripped down and approaching in our vulnerability and weakness, in our shyness, embarrassment, and disgrace (lack of grace).

For many years I was aware, intellectually, of the need to confess and approach God with a sense of need and brokenness, but this took on a new meaning when I came across the Myers-Briggs Type Indicator. Knowing my personality type helped me to understand where and how I needed to examine myself, and why I was unaware of so much. An understanding of it continues to sustain me in the process of self-knowledge and awareness. Prayer and reflection using these insights has let these words take on a new meaning: "Prayer gives a man the opportunity of getting to know a gentleman he hardly ever meets. I do not mean his maker, but himself."[8] Presumably it is the same for women!

> Something in me is stirring;
> I think it's the part of me
> that waits in lonely exile
> and yearns for a homeland.
>
> It's the hidden part of me
> that wanders aimlessly,
> stumbling in the dark,
> crying to be found.
>
> O God of exiles and strangers,
> find the homeless parts of me:
> guide them toward yourself,
> for you are my promised land.
>
> Take the stranger inside of me
> and find familiar soil for it.
> Keep me mindful of the Emmanuel,
> whose sojourn brought a glimpse of home.[9]

Knowing Me, Knowing God

Some people seem to repress not only the weak and embarrassing things that they can't handle, but also some of their richer and endearing qualities. There are many people who have protected themselves so well, for so long, that it is now difficult to reach the "real person." Their unconscious contains not only negative aspects, but also much that is positive and attractive and which, if it was allowed to develop, would enable them to become much more approachable and fulfilled.

It is likely that, because we are not ultimately in control of our shadow in the way that we are in control of our conscious self, there is a greater opportunity for God to use it to break through into our lives. That is one reason why we so often read in Scripture of God speaking to people in dreams, for when we are asleep we relax our control and allow other things to happen.[10] Seen this way, it then becomes essential to pay attention to this aspect of our personality. It will probably be a long and doubtless a painful journey that we have to embark on, but one full of surprises and abounding in opportunities for growth and rewards.

Understanding the shadow helps to explain why people's behavior, including our own, often comes as a surprise and we hear ourselves saying, "I really don't know what came over me, it wasn't like me at all." It was not like me, because I am usually in control of myself; and my shadow, with all its repressed baggage, is usually well locked away. It is when the lid pops open that behavior "out of character" manifests itself. The person who is always friendly and accepting, whose preferred function is Feeling, may suddenly reveal a mean, rather ruthless streak, and they may appear cold and unapproachable. A person whose dominant or auxiliary is Thinking may suddenly display behavior which appears totally irrational. They may flare off in a temper, totally unreasonably, or they may act in what appears to be a most bizarre and illogical manner. They are unable to control their Feeling side and so it suddenly bursts through to the front, unchecked by the restraints of thought and consideration. A person who prefers iNtuition and has that as their dominant may find that they have odd fantasies, and be horrified to recognize that all sorts of sexual impulses come to their mind. A dominant Senser may suffer from depression, finding no way out of what appears to be a difficult situation, or they may suddenly announce a solution to their problems which their friends find totally bizarre or worrying. They may suddenly announce that they are selling their belongings and going to live in France, for instance, even though no one in the family speaks French! What is happening in these cases is that a person's least-preferred function is suddenly bursting through in an uncontrolled or inappropriate manner.

The realization that we have another side to our personality, and that we are not entirely the person that we would have others believe us to be—nor are we really the person we would wish to be—can be a real step forward in our spiritual development. We are then reaching the point where we know that we have to offer to God not only our strengths and our talents, and not only our conscious awareness of the things that we have done which we should not have and our failure to do what we know we should have done. We are recognizing that we also have to hand over to God this wild and unacknowledged part of our personality, this veritable Pandora's box, containing all the repressed and forgotten things that we have accumulated over our entire lifetime. In such a situation we become aware of our need for grace.

A great many people find that they come to explore their shadow in mid-life or later. This is the time when people may realize that things which were appropriate and helpful to them when they were younger no longer seem so relevant in middle age. Jung said that things which worked in the first part of life do not work in the second, which is why people often have a crisis of some sort, or experience pain and confusion in mid-life.

Many people quite naturally come to use their less-preferred functions in their spiritual life, and are aware of the need to engage those parts of their personality which tend to be rather less developed. That may be one reason why, in completing the questionnaire in chapter 3, you may have come up with different letters from those which describe your personality type. There is often an acknowledgment that we need to bring our areas of weakness and vulnerability to God. While our less-preferred functions may be our weaker ones, that is not always the case, and we need to take care that we do not automatically assume that functions that are not our preferred functions are automatically crude and weak. We may have been operating with those functions well to the fore because of expectations placed upon us by our family or work situation, and so we may be skilled at using them even though they are not actually our preferred functions.

Perhaps it is best to reflect on the possibility that, when approaching spiritual matters it is likely that all of our functions are weak and inadequate, and that we handle them all rather clumsily.

The important thing to understand is that, when we feel "in control" we are inevitably putting up barriers, making it more difficult for us to be aware of the graciousness of God. This is why Paul discovered that our strength in God ultimately rests in weakness. It is when we are conscious of our own shortcomings and fragility, not in a morbid self-pitying way but consciously acknowledging the totality of our personality, that we tend to be most receptive to the promptings and presence of God's Spirit.

Coming to terms with our weakness, by way of acknowledging our shadow, is not an easy or comfortable process. It involves stripping down concepts, constructs, ideas, and beliefs which we have carefully built up over the years, and which we cling to in order to give meaning, a context, and security to our life. These may well be broken down without any assurance that they will be replaced. This "dark night of the soul" has been movingly portrayed by Jane Williams:

> It describes a time when we are made to realize that God is bigger than, different from, all our ways of knowing and speaking and praying. It is a time of considerable confusion and fear, when we are unlearning what we thought we knew, but have nothing to put in its place. All the things that seemed so reliable, about ourselves, our place in the world and in relation to God, are no longer certain, we no longer know what weight they will bear, and yet, if we cannot lean on them, we do not

know how to go forward. . . . If we are not prepared to unlearn the language and habits that confine God, then we cannot learn more about God. . . . The Christian tradition does have, built in, a strand that recognizes the importance of spiritual chaos. The dark night of the soul has to be described in negative terms, and is experienced as frightening and uncontrolled, and yet it is an experience of growth. . . . In the darkness, when we seem to have no knowledge of God at all, in the blankness when our language about God is taken from us, at those times when God seems least like God, our tradition helps us to know that God is actually breaking in, through the barriers of language and prayer, through the neat models that we have constructed to keep God safe and to harness God for our own use.[11]

I believe that the concept of the shadow is larger than the least-preferred functions revealed by the MBTI, but that these functions provide a very helpful way in to the subject. Similarly, the whole area of spirituality is much larger than issues of personality type and preferences; but an understanding of type can be very helpful in providing a framework, a context, and the tools for analysis when we are confronted by so great and mysterious a subject. It would be foolish to make exaggerated claims for the MBTI in the area of spiritual formation, but it would be equally sad to ignore the insights and help that it can provide for those who take the time and trouble to explore it.

Although she didn't include spirituality in her list of areas where an understanding of type might be of value, it is difficult to believe that Isabel Briggs Myers would not be the first to want to add it, for at the end of her book she says:

I have looked at the world from the standpoint of type for more than fifty years and have found the experience constantly rewarding. An understanding of type can be rewarding for society too. It is not too much to hope that wider and deeper understanding of the gifts and diversity may eventually reduce the misuse and non-use of those gifts. It should lessen the waste of potential. . . . Whatever the circumstances of your life, whatever your personal ties, work and responsibilities, the understanding of type can make your perceptions clearer, your judgments sounder, and your life closer to your heart's desire.[12]

The Personality of Jesus

One of the questions that I am almost always asked when running a workshop for a church group is "What was Jesus' personality type?" It is a difficult question to answer for a number of reasons.

It is always difficult trying to project modern instruments back into history. It is like asking what sort of car Jesus would have had if cars had been invented then, or would he have liked pop music? It is a problem when dealing with any historical figure. Would Henry VIII have played the French horn? Would Robin Hood have played soccer (presumably for Nottingham Forest!)? Would Florence Nightingale have preferred cooking by gas or electricity? We just do not know.

More seriously, it is difficult for us to know very much about the actual figure of Jesus. We have many stories about him, and we have accounts of the impact that he made upon many of the people he met, but these stories were all written down long after the events or conversations took place. In the last century and in the early years of this century, some scholars made a determined effort to try and discover "the historical Jesus" and write a modern biography of him. All such attempts failed to produce anything convincing.

The truth is that we do not have a written record about Jesus which primarily focuses upon him as a person. We have the Gospel records, written by people within the early church, with the purpose of sustaining faith and proclaiming his message, but the writers were not concerned with giving us the sort of detailed information that we, in our time, so often crave. Even the material that we do have is open to all sorts of critical debate and questioning; and the church does not have a universally agreed understanding of the Bible, apart from a general conviction that it is the Word of God. What such a phrase as that means is itself open to discussion, as we are reminded every so often when the media choose to spotlight some leading personality who expresses a view about the Bible which is not universally accepted and which is thought to be controversial. For the purpose of this chapter, I am taking the biblical narrative on face value. This is not the time or place to enter into detailed textual discussion.

While it is quite impossible for us to know how Jesus would have scored on a Myers-Briggs questionnaire, it is clear that he used all the functions described and explored by Myers and Briggs. This point is really crucial to understanding MBTI. The instrument stresses that it doesn't matter which type you are, for all the functions are of equal value and worth, and every person has gifts. Whatever type a person turns out to be, they will use all eight alternatives, even though they have a preference for some of them and will use them more than others. What is important is that we learn to operate in different ways, using different functions, so that we get to know what our preferences are, and use the appropriate function (whether dominant, auxiliary, third- or fourth-preferred) whatever situation we are in.

The incarnation made Jesus specific: he became human and therefore limited. He was born as a man and not as a woman; he grew to be a specific size and weight (although we have no idea what they were); he was a Jew rather than a European, North American, or African; and presumably, in our terms, he was of a certain personality type (and had a certain fingerprint pattern, as well, for that matter). These specific things about Jesus, some of which we know and some of which we are ignorant of, do not mean that he was not available to, representative of, or sympathetic to those who were different. While he will have been a specific personality type (though note the difficulty mentioned earlier of "projecting back" the idea of personality type), he will, in Myers-Briggs terms, have had to live and work and minister both as an Introvert and an Extrovert, as a Senser and also as an iNtuitive, as a Thinker and a Feeler, and finally as a Perceiver and also as a Judger. Thus he shared with us both the opportunities and the frustrations of each of those categories.

What follows can only be a most cursory and superficial exploration. It is not purporting to be a detailed or profound description of the character or personality profile of Jesus. What it does show, however, is that we can see from the Gospel stories how Jesus used different parts of his personality differently and appropriately, in different situations. It is an interesting exercise, and one that people can develop further. It offers us a new way of reading and reflecting on the Gospels.

It is quite simple to think of situations in which Jesus operated as an Introvert. The great wilderness experience is an example, where he went off alone at the beginning of his public ministry, to be tempted and to prepare himself for the work ahead. He needed to be alone, to have the time and space to think, and to wrestle with these thoughts. At the end of his ministry, in the Garden of Gethsemane, Jesus again chooses to be alone as he wrestles through the night with the agony of the decision that he must make. In the intervening period there are many instances of Jesus getting away from the crowds and spending time alone. No doubt it was during these periods that he "recharged his batteries," sorted out his thinking, and made space for God's guidance and strength to become clear to him. There is also the lovely story of the woman with the alabaster jar of expensive perfume[1] which she brings to anoint Jesus' head. He relaxes and lays back, and as she anoints him she is criticized by others for doing this when the ointment could have been sold and the money spent on the poor. Here is a classic tension between introverted honoring and anointing and extroverted activism and social engagement. In this instance Jesus scolds the woman's critics and reminds us that there is a time and a place for outward engagement and there is a time and a place for turning aside from external demands and focusing upon what might be described as "the still, small voice"—the inner conviction which takes precedence over the demands of external pressures. He then says that what this woman has done will be remembered throughout the ages, and so today we can still reflect upon that introverted act of homage.

There are many occasions, however, in which Jesus comes over to us not as an Introvert, but rather as an Extrovert. The very fact that he chose twelve disciples to be around him, to be his friends and companions, suggests a person who is gregarious and who enjoys the cut and thrust of discussion. Even when he has to go alone, to pray in Gethsemane, he asks for his friends to be nearby and to support him in prayer. Beyond the close circle of disciples, it is clear that Jesus had many friends, Mary, and Martha, and their brother Lazarus foremost among them. He talked with a wide range of people, and was known and identified by large crowds. One of the criticisms leveled against him was that he ate and drank with publicans and sinners. This image of a sociable, gregarious, wandering figure offers all sorts of extrovert suggestions. The dramatic entry into Jerusalem on Palm Sunday[2] could be said to be an extreme form of extroverted behavior! A great deal of his teaching was about social relationships, about the dynamic interaction between people. While much of it was within small groups, it is also clear that much of it was extremely public, and that vast crowds gathered to hear him. The picture emerges of a man who is stimulated by company, who responds to the pressures and opportunities that the outer world presents, and who finds a great deal of meaning and purpose in sharing his thoughts and ideas with others.

When we look at the Sensing-iNtuiting axis, we can again see that Jesus was able to operate effectively and appropriately at either end. He noticed small details, a common practice of Sensers. He was aware of the woman touching the hem of his garment; he noticed Zacchaeus in the branches of the tree; and Nathanael sitting in the shade of a fig tree. In his teaching, Jesus often encouraged people to be specific and to think of small details—"consider the lilies of the field"—and he reminded them that the very hairs on their head were numbered. He was aware of the practical problems when a large number of people followed him and did not have enough to eat, and he was quite specific about the details he gave to his disciples when asking them to prepare things for his entry into Jerusalem for the Passover. A considerable amount of detail is given in the New Testament about eating and drinking, and the institution of the Last Supper is a quite specific piece of detailed action. Glancing through the Gospels quickly, for instance when I am looking for a particular passage, I am time and again struck by how much of the material is specifically related to individual people and to particular happenings. There is a sense of immediacy and practicality about them, and within such a context Jesus quite easily and naturally assumes the personality of a Sensing person.

But the content of much of Jesus' teaching was the kingdom of God, and the kingdom is a theme which has enormous appeal to iNtuitives. The kingdom is concerned with the "big picture" of peace, justice, and righteousness; and Jesus shows himself to be a true iNtuitive when he speaks of the future, or when he poses questions. Time and time again he seems to get right to the heart of a matter, cutting through all the extraneous material, not getting bogged down with details so that he misses the point. He saw the potential in the most unsuspecting people, and was able to summon up in them amazing acts of heroism, dedication, and courage. Jesus was prepared to take risks. He challenged people to work things out for themselves: "but what do you think," he seems to be saying repeatedly. He was able to see beyond what other people could see, and so on several occasions could say words such as "if only you had eyes to see and ears to hear." Jesus strides across the pages of the New Testament as a man with a vision, a purpose, and an all-embracing understanding of the future which influenced virtually everything he did and said. Such a description would place him well within the ranks of the iNtuitives—and yet we know that he was also a Senser.

Perhaps the most obvious description that could be attached to Jesus is that of Feeler, for the Gospels are full of incidents in which his concern for people, his desire for peace—indeed his gift of peace—are fundamental and all-important. "Come to me, all who are weary and burdened, and I will give you rest"—this image of Jesus as the one who relieves us of our burdens of sin and guilt, who tends to our brokenness, and who heals and restores us, is basic to our understanding of him. He weeps over Jerusalem, he shows concern for the thief on the cross, he forgives those who brutally despise him, and he lays down his life for others. Jesus could be said to represent the basic Feeling type par excellence; he seems to be able to understand how others feel, he has time for them, he puts himself out for them, and nothing seems to be more important than meeting the needs of others. He heals the sick, searches out the lost, restores the penitent, and gives hope to those who feel themselves to be without hope. His reading of the Scriptures in the synagogue encompasses a Feeling approach to life—"The Spirit of the Lord is upon me, because he has anointed me to preach good news to the poor. He has sent me to proclaim freedom for the prisoners and recovery of sight for the blind. . . . Today this scripture is fulfilled."[3] The identification of Jesus with the Suffering Servant songs in Isaiah[4] only serves to reinforce this view.

It would be a mistake, however, to cast Jesus in a permanent Feeling image, a sort of grown-up "gentle Jesus meek and mild." For it is possible to detect a shaft of steel in his personality, and a detachment from what is going on around him which is sometimes surprising. Jesus can be seen to act as a Thinker. There is the story of his childhood appearance in the Temple, disputing with the elders there. He seems to have been unconcerned about the anxiety that his temporary disappearance had caused his mother and father, " 'Why were you searching for me?' he asked. 'Didn't you know I had to be in my Father's house?' "[5] There is a similar seeming disregard for his family when, in Matthew 12, we are told of an incident in which someone told Jesus that his mother and brothers were waiting outside wanting to speak to him, and Jesus replied, "Who is my mother, and who are my brothers?" and he goes on to say that "whoever does the will of my Father in heaven is my brother and sister and mother."[6] It is difficult to reconcile these apparently hurtful words with the Feeling-dominated Jesus of the previous paragraph. There is a commitment to truth which is all-important, and on more than one occasion Jesus warns his followers that it is a costly venture to become one of his disciples. Far from establishing harmony, he warns that discipleship may divide families and cause great pain and stress. He does not water down this cost of commitment, and so when the rich young man comes to him wanting to be a disciple but unable to face up to the cost of renouncing his fortune, we are told that Jesus, "sorrowing," watched him turn away, and he let him go. Soon after the moment of great insight at the transfiguration, when there must have been created a special bond between Jesus and his closest friends, he is able to turn on Peter saying, "Get thee behind me, Satan" when the disciple seeks to offer an easier road to Jesus than the one he feels that he must follow. Truth, objectivity, purpose, and integrity are the hallmarks of the Thinking personality, and they are to be seen in abundance in the character of Jesus.

When considering the Judging function we are reminded of the need for closure, of the value of tradition and authority, of order and reliability, of trust and faithfulness—all aspects which can be found in the ministry and life of Jesus. In Mark's Gospel he bursts onto the scene with a sense of urgency and purpose: "The time has come, the kingdom of God is near. Repent and believe the good news!" Jesus is conscious of a tradition, and sees himself continuing the ministry of John the Baptist. He goes back much further, to Elijah and, as the new lawgiver, he continues the work of Moses the old lawgiver. Matthew's Gospel is particularly concerned to show how Jesus saw himself within a particular tradition. He was a loyal and dependable friend, someone to turn to when in distress or afraid. Asleep in a boat when the weather turned stormy, the disciples woke Jesus up and looked to him to help them cope with a frightening situation. He was a man who had authority, an inner authority of his own, not like the authority of the scribes and Pharisees, and people listened to him and acted on his word. "Just say the word, and my daughter will be healed." He was a man who inspired confidence and trust, and people marveled at his words. He took responsibility for his actions, and he took upon himself the burdens and sins of others. There was clearly a great deal of J in his character.

But once again, that is not the whole story. Jesus was able to keep his options open. He seemed free to wander around the countryside, going where he wanted and seeming not to follow any clearly defined and specific pattern or route. He mixed with "undesirables," he was not prepared to take people as others found them, he would make his own decision. When he was criticized for picking corn on the sabbath he replied that the sabbath was made for man and not the other way round. Although he had a mission and was committed to it with a sense of urgency, he could also relax; he could spend time with his friends and be deflected by people or circumstances. The little incident with the Canaanite woman[7] is a good example of how he was open to new insight and was prepared to alter his perspective. The woman comes to him for help and the disciples want to turn her away. Jesus seems to agree with them, saying that he was sent only to the lost sheep of Israel, but the woman persists and kneels before him. Jesus tells her that it is not right to take children's bread and throw it to the dogs (hardly the conversation of an F!), but she counters that even the dogs eat the crumbs that fall from their master's table. Jesus is prepared to change his mind, and he replies, "Woman, you have great faith! Your request is granted." The woman's daughter was healed "from that very hour." That is the response of a person who is a P in terms of personality characteristics.

It is thus possible to see that Jesus operated in all the different functions and it is quite impossible for us to say that he preferred one to another. We too operate in all the functions, but because we prefer some to the others we often find it dif-

The Personality of Jesus

ficult to act appropriately in any given situation. We have a tendency to want to meet every person and every situation using our preferred functions, but sometimes it is more appropriate to use the other ones. Jesus seemed to know how to respond appropriately in whatever situation he found himself, and in that way he is a role model and an example for us all to follow.

7

Confounded by the Cross[1]

*H*ow might an understanding of personality type help in developing an appropriate personal spirituality? This epilogue is an extended example of how an understanding of type has helped me. I chose a popular hymn and reflected on it, seeing how the insights of personality type illuminated and expanded the text.

> When I survey the wondrous cross
> On which the Prince of Glory died,
> My richest gain I count but loss
> And pour contempt on all my pride.

The first thing that struck me about this verse was that it begins with me, where I am, and it recognizes that I have power and control over myself, my actions, and thoughts. I choose to look at the cross, and the hymn begins with what I choose to do. I look at the cross of Jesus and immediately my iNtuition comes to the fore (iNtuition is my dominant), and I reflect on the fact that it is a public cross, stuck up on a hillside for all to see. It is a cross for all people. You don't have to be a citizen or an insider to be confronted by this cross, for it is outside the city wall. You don't have to be a scholar, a philosopher, or one of the "in people," one of the privileged. You don't even have to be religious; in fact it sometimes helps not to be, for religion has a particular way of obscuring our sight of the cross. It was the Jewish theologian Martin Buber who said "nothing obscures the face of God like religion." Most of all, you don't have to be good, righteous, or successful. There is no one who may not come and look at the cross. It is there for the thief, it is there for Peter who failed the test of friendship, it is there for the mother whose heart is broken, it is there for the cynic and the scornful, it is there for the penitent and for the faithful. That was the situation in Palestine, and that is the situation today, for you, and for me.

My iNtuition has grasped hold of this idea of the universality of the cross, and I am developing it, drawing on specifics, which would appeal to the Senser. I can now develop it for the Feeler, making it subjective and associated with the desire for peace and harmony.

Are you lonely? The cross is there. Are you carrying a fear or burden that troubles you? The cross is there. Are you afraid of dying? The cross is there. Are you afraid of living? The cross is there. Do you feel that no one understands you . . . are you tired and weary . . . are you disillusioned . . . have you worked too hard, loved too much, given your all—and yet still find yourself unsatisfied, restless, and not at peace with yourself and the world? The cross is there. On the other hand, perhaps you are bursting with joyfulness at the splendor of creation. Perhaps you have experienced a love and a tenderness which cradles your vulnerability and whispers to your inner being that all is well and all will be well (the text is now embracing Sensing). For you also, the cross is there. It is there in our times of strength and in our times of weakness, in our joys and in our sorrows, in our faith and in our doubts. It is there for all of us, for all time and for all situations (the Senser requires specifics and the iNtuitive responds to the big, overall scene).

The text now moves on to engage the Thinking process, which raises questions about the words of the hymn. So we survey the wondrous cross, on which the Prince of Glory died. The very idea jars. There is a sense of dissonance and disharmony, for what sense are we to make of something so ghastly and abhorrent, and what has it to do with glory? It is this non-sense, this dislocation of rational thinking, that takes us by surprise. It is this that makes us realize that, when looking at the cross, we have to suspend all those patterns of thinking which we have developed to carry us through life. Now that is really difficult for people who pride themselves on their power of rational thought, who have developed their critical faculties and who have grown to trust their reasonable, coherent, and common sense approach to life. This is the struggle that people whose preference is Thinking have to face when confronted by issues of faith.

Perhaps for Thinkers this is the greatest pride: the pride which the hymn speaks of in its fourth line. For what is our greatest pride? When I thought about this question I came to the conclusion that I cling to, and seem to need above all else, my ability to think—to formulate and to make sense of my surroundings. And this is precisely what is of no use to me when I look at the cross. All the sophistication of thought, all the awareness of theories and formularies, all my intellectual and critical faculties leave me helpless and de-skilled in the face of the cross, and I am left to pour contempt on all my pride, for it has been exposed and found wanting.

That which I count to be of such great importance is unable to comprehend the meaning or significance of such suffering, unable to make sense of a God who becomes known by and through dereliction. The hymn says that I pour contempt on all my pride, but that is actually an inappropriate response. God would not have us harbor contempt in our hearts, and it is neither healthy nor right for us to hold our rationality in contempt. So often we resort to contempt when confronted by situations, or people, or events, that we can neither understand nor cope with. We choose to look at the cross, and as we look we denigrate, pour contempt on, or in some other way despite that part of us which makes it difficult for us to cope. But it is far better for us to understand and accept those parts of us which we find difficult to acknowledge, our shadow, than to be negative, scornful, or contemptuous about them.

The first verse of the hymn has limitations. In this verse we are still well and truly in control of the situation. Although it tries to focus upon the cross, it begins with me and it ends with what I propose to do about things.

Knowing Me, Knowing God

Forbid it Lord, that I should boast
Save in the death of Christ my God
All the vain things that charm me most
I sacrifice them to his blood.

The first two verses are rooted in Scripture and take their inspiration from Paul's letters to the Philippians. That is good for Sensers. They like ideas to be rooted in actual situations, to have a specific point of reference which can be called upon and checked out. But again, iNtuition can use this as a jumping-off point to reflect, for example, on the many important and moving letters that have been written from prisons around the world, by Paul himself, Bonhoeffer, Martin Luther King, and many others.

In Philippians Paul recalls the boasting he could do, but says that he has "written off" such "assets" because of Christ. All he cares for is to know Christ, experience the power of his resurrection, and to share in his sufferings.[2] He might have continued "therefore I rot away in this prison," but what he actually wrote was "The Lord is near. Do not be anxious . . . but in everything, by prayer and petition, with thanksgiving, present your requests to God.[3]

By any stretch of the imagination, that is a remarkable message to come out of prison, and it turns our established understanding of things upside down. Things are not as they seem to be. Things have never been as they seem to be within the Christian tradition. That is what makes it so powerful, magnetic, and fearful. There actually is a tension, a polarity, a built-in contradiction between the world as it is now as humankind has made it, and the world as purposely created and sustained by God. This tension is nowhere more starkly and vividly illustrated than by the events in Jerusalem on that first Good Friday.

Paul, in prison, found in his vulnerability and his captivity an awareness of God which made everything else that he had, and everything that he was, seem as nothing. All the things which the prevailing culture had persuaded him were important—birth, lineage, education, righteousness, and citizenship—and all the prizes that the prevailing culture had set before him—status, purpose, respect, security, and esteem—all these things he counted as nothing. They were all to be set aside for the riches that he found in Christ. For us, the question to be answered is "what are the marks of captivity to the prevailing culture that can be found on us?" To what extent have we allowed ourselves, probably unwittingly, to be conditioned and formed by the standards, values, and expectations of the society in which we live? What has been repressed and forced into our unconscious, to become part of our shadow? What are the marks of respectability, the signs of security, and the interpretations of society that drive a wedge into our hearts and seek to separate us from the claims and values of the reign of God? What, in the words of the hymn, are the vain things that charm us most?

Who was being crucified? A good man? A political rabble-rouser? A blasphemer? An innocent, perhaps naive, wandering craftsman? All these answers have a certain amount to commend them, and it would be possible to build up a case and argue for each one of them. The Thinker would do this objectively, standing outside the situation and looking on; the Feeler would do it subjectively, imagining him or herself to be part of the situation. The answer that is virtually impossible to argue, sustain, or even comprehend, is that it was God who was being crucified.

To claim that God was being crucified is to contradict virtually everything that humankind has ever meant, conceived, or desired by the word "God." We are being asked to abandon our rationality and take a leap, landing we know not where. This poses enormous problems for Thinkers, Sensers, and Judgers. No wonder we cling to what we already know, and persevere with what we can control.

All this seems most unreasonable. It does not fit our convenient view of the world, but then, the idea of God on a cross is absurd. The dialogue with the cross is a dialogue with doubt and uncertainty, with open-ended commitment, and with a way of life that stands in contradistinction to the prevailing way of looking at society. That is how an iNtuitive Perceiver views the challenge; would a Senser and a Judger need to rephrase it in more "type-appropriate" words, or do these words ring true for all types?

Knowing Me, Knowing God

These are some of the issues raised by the second verse of the hymn, but note, we are still in control. The responsibility for action still rests with us, and we make the decision to replicate the sacrifice of Christ by sacrificing the things which are important to us.

> See from his head, his hand, his feet
> Sorrow and love flow mingled down
> Did e'er such love and sorrow meet
> Or thorns compose so rich a crown?

The third verse is completely different from all the others. First of all, and most importantly, we have lost control. In the first two verses we, as individuals, are essential to its purpose, and we have control over what is happening. In this verse there is no room for me. It is not concerned with what I think or do. It moves onto a new plane altogether. We are onlookers, bystanders, the passive mass of humanity somehow withdrawn from the action as the central characters of the drama move into their final scenes. The narration has slipped out of our hands because we are unable to grasp its significance, unable to comprehend its true meaning, and unable to affect its course.

We live in a world which is broken; a world which is not yet perfect, not in harmony with itself. The image appeals to the Senser, the reasoning to the Thinker, the lack of harmony to the Feeler, and the global scope to the iNtuitive. Sometimes the world appears to be getting worse as we destroy its beauty, waste its resources, and disregard the cries of pain and anguish which come from the weak, vulnerable, and voiceless. At other times we catch glimpses of hope as we see intimations of what might come to be someday. We have tantalizing trailers, as it were, of forthcoming attractions. These include visions of the reign of God; of a time when the promises of God will be manifest, made concrete, shared, and enjoyed by the whole of creation. However, for most of the time we are all too aware of the brokenness and dislocation of our world; of war and hunger, pestilence and tragedy, of disease and human greed, of pain and sorrow, of dying and of caricatures of living. We hear too much about heartache and betrayal. So often in these situations we do not know how to act. We do the best that we can, but we feel inadequate, pushed to the sidelines, to the periphery, and left to observe as the human drama unfolds, just as we are in the third verse of the hymn.

Whether the image in our mind when we think of the sorrow and suffering in the world is that of a fighter plane—screaming through the air and dropping its expensive load of death and destruction on helpless people; or whether it is of a loved one, confined to a bed of pain and teetering on the edge of life and death—the response is the same: a feeling of helplessness, inadequacy, and vulnerability. And where is God?

It is not that we want a heavenly super-daddy to absolve us from the obligations of living responsibly, with each other and with the created order. But where is God when it becomes painfully obvious that we, and others, have failed to live graciously, lovingly, and compassionately despite our determined efforts? How do we reconcile what we see and hear with what we say that we believe? (These are real questions for Thinkers to ask, and perhaps one reason why they very often fail to stay in our congregations.)

The voice of faith replies that God is there, on the ground, with the helpless people as the bombs fall on them. He is there with our dying loved ones. He is there, with the pot-bellied, spindle-legged, fly-infested orphan child in the refugee camp. He is there with the cancer-ridden, emaciated, drug-filled, helpless person on the bed surrounded by flowers and "get well" cards. He is there with the tear-stained betrayed wife or husband, or with the old, wandering person with dementia. He is there wherever people are crying out "Why?" And whether God is perceived as he or she, as "it" or as a blank-shaped question, the reality of a troubled yet dependable presence is there. Sharing, holding, embracing, weeping, and suffering, within and alongside creation. This conviction is at the heart of Christian believing. We believe in a God who allowed himself to be pushed out onto the periphery of life, and who allows himself still to be unceremoniously ignored, marginalized, trampled on, and humiliated, and who therefore understands what it means to be in those situations where life seems to pass people by.

God is a God who allowed himself to be crucified so that, from that time on until the end of eternity, those who experience crucifixion in one form or another in their own daily living might know that their situation is understood and that their crying is heard. (This relates to Sensing and iNtuition, to Feeling and Thinking.)

The event of the cross was also the experience of separation. A lonely, mystifying, and painful separation. A separation that made no sense. A separation which left one party stretched out in agony and the other party restrained and inactive, unwilling or unable to intervene until the whole drama was over. Did e'er such love and sorrow meet? From that moment onwards a new perspective has been given to us which we can draw on and take comfort from in our own experiences of separation.

As we stand by and watch we have no words to say, no explanations to give, no frame of reference which can make sense of this non-sense which is played out before our eyes. It is as though our Senses, our Feeling, our Thinking, and our iNtuition are numbed, as though our shadow is revealed and all of it is poured out, and we can only stand and watch, naked and with no justification or explanation.

> Were the whole realm of nature mine
> That were an offering far too small
> Love so amazing, so divine
> Demands my soul, my life, my all.

Many people find it difficult to come to terms with a gospel which does not fit into the conceptual and intellectual framework that has been prepared for that part of their experience called "God," or for those aspects of life which can be regarded as "spiritual." Thinkers especially will have trusted their intellect and reflected on their experiences working to make sense of the world. And yet a confrontation with suffering love, whether in the crucifixion of Jesus or in daily experiences here and now, smashes all the plans, ideas, and defenses that have been built up.

Confounded by the Cross

God comes to us from beyond, from the outside. We cannot conceive or create God, though many have tried to do so, but he comes to us in disturbing ways, in threatening and challenging circumstances, very often through our shadow. He comes to us in the passion of Jesus in a costly, painful, and unexpected way: he comes through brokenness, through pain and suffering, through rejection and disappointment, through misunderstanding and betrayal. An understanding of personality type is not a pain-free passage to God; it is not an anesthetized spirituality which bypasses the need for brokenness.

And yet there is hope. There is hope for all who fail and are misunderstood. There is hope for those who witness, experience, or even cause pain and suffering. There is hope for those who know the feeling of being lost, or the experience of shattered dreams and broken promises. Words are inadequate to express this experience of being enfolded and sustained in brokenness. To be able to describe this love adequately is to fail to understand it, for it lies beyond comprehension, and can only be known in our innermost being, and at a level and depth beyond words.

In the earlier verses of the hymn we reflected on our richest gains and the vain things that charm us most, but now we leave far behind that pernickety small-minded and individualistic review of our lives. We move into a totally different situation. We are not looking inward and picking on negative aspects of our life and agreeing to offer them up. Instead we are looking at the vastness and beauty of the whole of creation and offering that to God. Were the whole realm of nature mine, that were an offering far too small. God does not demand the petty peccadilloes of my soul, but the whole of my being, and nothing that I have is sufficiently big enough or good enough, in itself, to offer up in praise, thanksgiving, and adoration.

The cross is central to Christian understanding. It is a pathway into the very nature of God, a window into the heart of God. It stands outside of ourselves, and so we can approach it via our extroverted processes, and yet we are called to internalize it, so that it becomes part of our being that we can feed on via our introverted processes. It becomes for us not only a specific cross, erected in a certain geographical spot on a certain day, but also a representative cross symbolizing the pain and suffering of a whole creation. Our feelings cannot be unmoved when we reflect upon the pain and the distress, the wickedness and the need for forgiveness; but our minds are challenged and a thousand questions forever appear as we try to make sense of something as nonsensical as a crucified God. We seek to find order, and meaning, and structure; and need all the strengths that Judgment can bring. But we are forever being taken by surprise, and reminded that we need to live in a provisional manner, and that change will always be near at hand; and we need to be able to live at ease with the Perceiving function of our personality.

We know that, however carefully we marshal our thoughts and prepare our hearts, we carry with us a great unconscious shadow. It contains our repressed desires and emotions, and so much that we are unable to acknowledge or face up to. That too needs to be part of the offering that we make, for it is just as much part of us as the strengths and skills that we are proud to present.

In the journey to God, it is not only helpful to be honest about ourselves; it is in the end essential. Understanding personality type is part of that process. Knowing me is part of the process of knowing God.

Spirituality
Questionnaire Chart

Transfer the figures from the grid on page 54 onto the chart below.

Total in box 1———Extrovert

Total in box 2———Introvert

Therefore preference* is Extrovert/Introvert

Total in box 3———Sensing

Total in box 4———INtuitive

Therefore preference* is Sensing/INtuitive

Total in box 5———Feeling

Total in box 6———Thinking

Therefore preference* is Feeling/Thinking

Total in box 7———Judging

Total in box 8———Perceiving

Therefore preference* is Judging/Perceiving

*Whichever score is higher

You now have four figures which can be said to describe your spiritual preferences—but only in the most general of ways. Chapter 4 looks at what each of these preferences implies, and it may be that as you read these you will want to alter your "pro-file." It is much more likely that your own assessment of what your preferences are, in the light of the descriptions and dis-cussions which follow, is more reliable than the profile derived from the questionnaire. I hope, though, that the questionnaire served its purpose in opening up for you the wide variety of responses that can be made to a range of questions about spir-ituality, and that this helps you to explore the subject with a greater freedom and sense of curiosity.

Notes

Prologue

1. See Isaiah 45:15.
2. D. Hammarskjold, Markings (Faber 1964).
3. See T. Merton, Thoughts in Solitude (Burns and Oates 1958).
4. Gerard W. Hughes, Oh God, Why? (Bible Reading Fellowship 1993).

1. Spirituality—A Technicolored Dreamcoat?

1. C. J. Keating, Who We Are Is How We Pray (Mystic, CT, Twenty-Third Publications 1987).
2. B. Duncan, Pray Your Way (DLT, 1993).

2. Understanding Personality Type

1. This is linked to the Muslim (Sufi) tradition but has, in recent years, become quite popular within the Christian church. See, for instance, The Enneagram and Prayer—Discovering Our True Selves Before God by Barbara Metz and John Churchill (Dimension Books Inc., Denville, New Jersey 1987) and, from the same publisher, Nine Portraits of Jesus—Discovering Jesus Through the Enneagram by Robert Nogosek.
2. MBTI and Myers-Briggs Type Indicator are registered trademarks of Consulting Psychologists Press Inc.
3. Malcolm Goldsmith and Martin Wharton, Knowing Me—Knowing You (SPCK 1993). In chapter 2 the theory behind the MBTI is explained more fully than space allows in this book.
4. Isabel Briggs Myers, Gifts Differing (Consulting Psychologists Press Inc. 1980).
5. Answers: s, n, f, f, f, n, s.
6. Peter Briggs Myers in the Introduction to Knowing Me—Knowing You.

7. Mark A. Pearson, Why Can't I Be Me? (Chosen Books—a division of Baker Book House, Grand Rapids, Michigan 1992).

3. A Spirituality Questionnaire

1. See the work done by W. Bridges in The Character of organizations: Using Jungian Type in Organizational Development (Consulting Psychologists Press Inc. 1992).

4. Spirituality and Personality

1. Mark 12:29-31 (Good News Bible).
2. Lloyd Edwards, How We Belong, Fight and Pray (Alban Institute 1993).
3. Samuel Miller, quoted in John Ackerman's Finding Your Way—Personalized Practices for Spiritual Growth (Alban Institute 1993).
4. Duncan, op. cit.
5. Brian Keenan, An Evil Cradling (Vintage Edition, Arrow Publishing 1993). Used with permission of Random House UK Ltd.
6. Vincent J. Donovan, The Church in the Midst of Creation (SCM 1989).
7. A prayer by Joyce Gray in response to "To Weavers Everywhere" by M. Rienstra in a WCC Women's Newsletter, used at a commissioning service for Alastair and Fiona Hulbert as they left Edinburgh for Brussels, August 1991.
8. It used to be common practice to speak of the kingdom of God, and kingdom theology, but some recent writers have argued that this language is no longer appropriate—that to speak of kingdoms is to speak of kings, and that is a masculine image. Admittedly the New Testament speaks in these terms but, they argue, it is more helpful and courteous to speak of the "reign of God" wherever possible.
9. C. G. Jung, Psychological Types, The Collected Works, Vol. 6 (Princeton University Press 1971).
10. The Independent, 8 December 1988.
11. David Jenkins, "Evangelization and Culture," a lecture given at the 1988 Lambeth Conference and printed in Thinking Mission (USPG, January 1990).
12. Wildgoose publications.
13. Sheila Cassidy, Sharing the Darkness (DLT 1988).
14. W. Barclay, The Lord's Supper (SCM 1967).
15. Haddon Willmer in Moule, The Origin of Christology, and quoted in Prickett's Godspells (Book Guild Ltd. 1992).
16. Eric James, The Voice Said, Cry! (SPCK 1994).
17. Duncan, op cit.
18. Johannes Tauler, quoted in Henry C. Simmons, In the Footsteps of the Mystics (Paulist Press 1992).

19. Eugene H. Peterson, The Contemplative Pastor: Returning to the Art of Spiritual Direction (Eerdmans 1993).
20. Donovan, op cit.

5. The Shadow

1. Keenan, op cit.
2. Terry Waite, Taken on Trust (Hodder and Stoughton 1993).
3. Robert Bly, A Little Book on the Human Shadow, 1988, published in Britain by Element, 1992.
4. William A. Miller, Make Friends with Your Shadow—How to Accept and Use Positively the Negative Side of Your Personality (Augsburg Publishing House, Minneapolis 1981).
5. M.-L von Franz, Shadow and Evil in Fairytales (Spring Publications Inc., Dallas 1974).
6. See, for example, the Jung and Spirituality series published by the Paulist Press, New Jersey.
7. Robert Repicky OSB, Jungian Typology and Christian Spirituality in The Way, vol. 42 (1983).
8. William Inge quoted in God: What the Critics Say, edited by Martin Wroe (Spire, Hodder and Stoughton 1992).
9. Excerpted from May I Have This Dance? by Joyce Rupp OSM. Copyright 1992 by Ave Maria Press, Notre Dame, IN 46556. Used with permission of the publisher.
10. See James A. Hall, The Unconscious Christian: Images of God in Dreams (Paulist Press 1993).
11. Jane Wiliams in "Mothers, Chaos and Prayer" in Mirror to the Church: Reflections on Sexism, ed. Monica Furlong (SPCK 1988).
12. Isabel Briggs Myers, op cit.

6. The Personality of Jesus

1. Matthew 26:6f; Mark 14:3f; Luke 7:37f.
2. Matthew 21:1-11.
3. Luke 4:16-21.
4. There are four songs in Isaiah, quoted in Matthew 12:18-21 with reference to Jesus. Isaiah 42:1-4 (7 or 9); 49:1-6 (7 or 13); 50:4-9 (or 11); 52:13–53:12. The notes of the NIV Study Bible say of these "He Is 'Israel' in its ideal form. The nation was to be a kingdom of priests (Exodus 19:6), but the Messiah would be the high priest who would atone for the sins of the world. Cyrus was introduced in Isaiah 41 as a deliverer from Babylon, but the servant would deliver the world from the prison of sin." (Hodder and Stoughton 1987).
5. Luke 2:49.
6. Matthew 12:48-50.
7. Matthew 15:21-28.

7. Confounded by the Cross

1. Because this reflection is based on a passion hymn, it inevitably focuses on suffering. There is more to Christian faith than suffering and weakness, and other emphases would obviously have come to the fore had I chosen a different hymn to illustrate the process. This material has formed the basis for a Three Hour service at St. John's, Princes Street, Edinburgh.
2. Philippians 3:10.
3. Philippians 4:5-7.

Further acknowledgments

Chapter 4

"Lord of the Dance" and "Every Star Shall Sing a Carol" by Sydney Carter. Reproduced by permission of Hope Publishing Co., Carol Stream, IL 60188.